HORSECARS AND COBBLESTONES

By Sophie Ruskay

ILLUSTRATIONS BY CECIL B. RUSKAY

South Brunswick

New York: A. S. Barnes and Company
London: Thomas Yoseloff Ltd

© 1948 by Sophie Ruskay

New edition published 1973 by A. S. Barnes and Co., Inc.

Library of Congress Catalogue Card Number: 72-6376

A. S. Barnes and Co., Inc.
Cranbury, New Jersey 08512

Thomas Yoseloff Ltd
108 New Bond Street
London W1Y OQX, England

ISBN 0-498-01301-4

Printed in the United States of America

CONTENTS

1

THE HOUSE

IT WAS lonely in the great big parlor that late winter afternoon. I was all by myself on the floor, practicing at the big shining black piano. Emma, our Polish girl, was singing in the kitchen below. I could hear her whenever I stopped banging the piano. She was enjoying herself, while I had to do the scales, C major, A major, F major, then the minor scales, fingers stumbling here, racing there, anything to finish.

At last I closed the exercise book. What a relief! Now for the *Piece*, the Faust "March." The teacher was coming the next day, so I simply had to learn it. I stretched my fingers for the big chords, counting out loud, "one, two, three, four—one, two, three, four."

The heavy draperies at the tall windows let only a little sun trickle through and made queer shadows. I could see them out of the corner of my eye. One, two, three, four . . . I rushed to the end of the Piece and banged the piano shut. I was through at last. I picked up the coat, hat and muffler lying in a heap nearby, and as I ran to escape from the room I saw myself in the tall mirror. I stopped. Such a solemn, funny, little face, pale, large gray eyes, brown thick hair in two braids and such ugly ears.

The room had become darker—goodness, could fairies or hobgoblins really come out from behind that shiny glass? "Of course not," I said out loud to give myself courage, "that was only a story in my last fairy book!" I slammed the big mahogany door and ran out to join my friends playing in the street.

It was a pretty street, in a quiet old-fashioned way, as all New York was fifty years ago. We had a nice house on East Broadway and had lived there ever since I was born. We did not occupy the whole house but only the basement and parlor floor. The three other floors were occupied by tenants who paid rent to my Mama and Papa and were our very good friends, besides. But the back yard was our very own to play in except on the days when it was crisscrossed by lines holding up our enormous wash. In the back yard we often settled our disputes in our own way. When I was "mad" at Mary or Lizzie, we naturally didn't talk to each other, even though we were sitting next to each other. We would converse through a real or mythical go-between. "Tell her I won't have anything to do with such a story-teller. She didn't win that game of jacks, because she touched in *twosies*," and this would go on and on until we weren't "mad" at each other any longer.

Part of the yard had been newly cemented to keep us from tracking dirt through the house. In the center of the yard from late spring to early fall there bloomed a bed of flowers bordered by bright red geraniums. Tall shrubs of Rose of Sharon screened off the fence of the neighbor's yard. It was, no doubt, a hideous affair judged by our taste in gardens today, but to me and my friends it was beautiful.

A great event was the arrival of a large wooden swing. Mama cautioned us to swing on it very gently. We were content to do just that for about a week until the novelty wore off. Then I invented a game I called "playing gymnasium." I planted my feet on the arms of the seat, grasped the spindly rail overhead and, with a mighty heave, swung my legs to where my hands were holding the rail. I let go my hands and swung just from my knees. Dangling upside down, seeing everything topsy-turvy, was great sport, until one of my friends spoiled everything by falling and breaking her arm. Mama, to placate the girl's angry mother, had the swing carted away.

Our parlor was long and narrow, with golden-haired cherubim painted on the high-vaulted ceiling. Then there were Mama's and Papa's room and an extension jutting out into the sunny back yard, which was occupied by two younger brothers. Connecting with it was another room, in which the most important object was a folding bed on which two of the older boys slept. In the daytime it served as a sofa, that is, when it consented to fold up; often it was quite temperamental. It created a considerable stir on one very solemn occasion, the first night of Passover.

Papa was half way through reading the Hagada, the recital of the Exodus from Egypt, when it was suddenly discovered that Ben had been surreptitiously sipping wine from the large silver cup set apart for the prophet Elijah. He was angrily sent from the table and ordered to bed. He protested; he insisted that he had only wanted to see what Elijah would do about it. Mama merely pointed her finger in the direction of the bedroom and said, "It's your luck it's a *yuntof* (a holiday) tonight or I would let you know not only what Elijah would do, but also what I will not fail to do when the *yuntof* is over." Ben went meekly off to the bedroom. Prayers were resumed and peace reigned once more at the table. Suddenly a howl came from the room containing the sofa-bed. The cries became muffled, then stopped altogether. There could be no mistaking the cause. Papa in his white cap, followed by Mama, the rest of us, and even the two guests, rushed from the table and helped extricate the imprisoned boy. That ended the sofa's career as a bed. Mama decided it would be less costly to her health and peace of mind to get rid of it, and buy a conventional bed.

Downstairs, in the front room facing the street, was the dining-room, where we also did our lessons. There was a dark bathroom to wash and bathe in. The toilet, commonly referred to, for some strange reason of delicacy, as a water-closet, was in the still darker hall; this was a great advance over the other houses in the neighborhood which had theirs in the yard.

Off the kitchen was a sort of study where my two oldest brothers slept and where they galloped through their morning prayers at record speed. There, too, after the boys had finished this ritual, waited the patient, emaciated *melamed* (teacher) who came at eight o'clock to teach me my Hebrew letters. As for Emma, the "girl" she had her own little cubby-hole.

I liked the kitchen best of all. Its windows looked out upon the back yard. A huge copper boiler gleamed next to the coal range, warm and friendly. The kitchen was always rich with delicious smells as soup bubbled in the big pot or crumb-covered yeast cakes slowly baked in the oven. And in the kitchen was Emma. After looking with a practiced eye at the cakes, she continued her ironing. With a thick wad of cloth in the palm of her hand, she picked up the flatiron from the stove, tested its heat by placing it perilously near her face or by spitting on it, and then continued to press the ruffles on my pinafores or Mama's petticoats with their wide embroidery flounces. Sometimes, as a special treat, she allowed me to iron the dish towels, while she sat down to rest. I would ask her to tell me again about the old country, about the goats and pigs she used to care for.

"America, it is good," she would say. She was learning to speak English but struggled to find the words. "The *pan* (the master) no work, not like here, not like Mama, Papa. Me, me work, carry all water to drink, to cook. Me, me milk cows, do everything, like man."

I looked admiringly at her strong squat figure, her smiling pockmarked face. "And what happened to the little calf whose Mama died?" I asked. "You didn't finish telling me about it."

I listened, enthralled. Suddenly an angry flow of Polish reminded me that I had forgotten I was ironing, and that I had burnt a large brown hole in Mama's best dish towel.

2

HOME LIFE

LARGE FAMILIES were the rule fifty years ago, seven, eight, ten, even twelve children were common. We were seven. There were three boys older than I, Abe, Harry and Ephie, and three boys younger, Sidney, Ben and David. I was in the middle, the only girl.

What I remember most clearly were the winter mornings and Mama. While we were washing and dressing, Mama would come in, already fully dressed, lending a hand here and there, braiding my tangled hair, giving orders to Emma, who would be helping the younger ones into their long flannel drawers. I wore them too, down to my ankles, and they were fiery red. I don't know why they had to be red, but I suppose it gave the illusion of greater warmth.

"David, come here, darling, sit on this chair and Mama will fix your curls." Mama wet the brush and deftly wound each curl around her forefinger, smacked it into place with the brush while she beguiled the recalcitrant David with

information about the shorn glory of his brother. "You
know, your brother Sidney was nearly five before I could
bring myself to cut his curls and when I did they were
so beautiful, we framed them. They hang downstairs on
the wall." Mama raised her voice, "Emma, I forgot to tell
you that I put the soup on and don't let the chicken fall
to pieces the way you did last time. Push the pot over to
the side so it cooks slowly and don't forget to close the
damper after the stove gets hot. Don't think because we
have a cellar full of coal we are millionaires. Waste not,
want not, I always say." Emma nodded her head in agree-
ment although she understood little of what Mama was
saying, but she gathered the meaning from Mama's smile
and gestures aided by a helpful word or two in Polish.

Mama straightened up the tumbled room. Her hat was
now on her head. The moment had come which we children
dreaded. Mama was about to leave us to go to the shop,
a vague place where Papa had already gone. To be sure,
she would come back for lunch but then only to leave us
again. We never seemed to get used to it. The wrench of
parting tore our hearts. We would wail in chorus, "Mama
do you love me?" Mama, clutching her bag and coat,
assured us again and again that she did, then disappeared
through the big front door.

We would get a last glimpse of her at the parlor window which looked out on the street. At the corner she
turned and waved to us, our faces pressed against the
window pane. She raised her finger to signal the driver
of the little horsecar. She jumped on the step. Mama
was no sylph, she was built on generous lines, but she
was swift in all her movements. The car bells tinkled,

the horses broke into a smart trot and she was gone. We hurried back to our breakfast and I to a half hour of Hebrew study with the teacher who had been waiting wearily in the basement. Then all of us, except the oldest and the youngest, were off to school.

Abe, then nearly fifteen, had already left with Papa. Blonde and stocky, full of a sense of importance at being the eldest, he considered himself a man of the world as he stalked out of the house each morning at seven, trying hard to keep up with Papa's long stride. He had been going to the shop with Papa since his graduation from school and his *Bar Mitzvah* (confirmation), both accomplished at thirteen. But this did not mean that going to business freed him from Mama's influence and her desire that he "improve each shining hour." After supper, like the rest of us, regardless of talent or interest, he had to study music. But the Talmud class he willingly attended several evenings a week. He prided himself on being the scholar of the family, and any refusal on the part of the younger boys to do his bidding was followed by so many texts from the holy books that they usually consented, if only to stem the flow of so much learning.

Harry was dark-skinned like Papa and myself, with a thin aquiline nose, and blue eyes set in a sensitive face. His health was a cause of endless worry to Mama. Her concern over Harry probably explains why he was her favorite, although she never admitted it. "I have no favorite," she would protest. "What kind of a mother has favorites?"

"Why then," I thought, "do you always speak of 'my Harry,' never of 'my Abe' or 'my Ephie'?"

But we were not jealous of Harry's place in Mama's affection, and silently admitted the justice of it. When Mama wanted anything, whether it was an errand to the grocer or someone to accompany her on a tedious trip to the factory, it was Harry who was first on his feet, long before we others shifted lazily from our seats.

Ephie, our abbreviation for the imposing Biblical name of Ephraim, was very handsome with Mama's steel blue eyes, black hair and slightly turned-up nose. When he was about seven or eight years old, he was racing one afternoon with some boys down our dark cellar steps. He fell and cut a horrible gash under his chin. As a result of the accident he developed a slight stutter. It became worse whenever he was angered or provoked, a fact of which we others took sly advantage.

Once, after an incoherent sputtering, one of us derisively called him "mecheche." Mama, quick as a flash, appeared from the next room and gave a resounding slap to the culprit, "Shame on you, to make fun of him!" Then she turned to Ephie and said, "Believe me, you will yet talk as well if not better than any of them. You must just have patience. When you are older you will go to a special class. They only have them at night, uptown. I spoke to your principal—he's a wonderful man. You know what he told me? There was a man who spoke far worse than you and he became the greatest orator in the world. I am speaking the truth, I should live so long. And how did he do it? Your principal, Mr. Keene, explained how. He put pebbles in his mouth to force himself to speak slowly. The main thing is not to get excited." She cast an angry look in our direction.

"Moses stuttered," I ventured, fresh from my newly gleaned Bible lore, "but he had Aaron to speak for him."

"I don't expect him to become a Moses, not even a Daniel Webster," Mama replied with her usual quickness. "It will be enough if he becomes a good businessman."

I was not much older than six when the teacher came every morning before school to teach me Hebrew. Once I asked Mama why I had to take these lessons so early in the day. Mama carefully explained, "Your brothers go to *cheder* (Hebrew school), where they study after public school, but there are no such places for girls. Where would we find a *rebbi* who would be willing to come in the afternoon? You don't want to grow up into an ignoramus, do you? You have to learn to read from the prayer book, to say your night-prayers. You will learn to translate a little from the *Chumish* (the Five Books of Moses). More we do not expect. Everybody, even a child, must make an early start if one wants to accomplish something in this world. Soon you'll be taking piano lessons."

"I don't want to take piano lessons," I objected.

"What do you know as to what you want or don't want?" she answered. "Do I expect you to become a Paderewski—or even to play the way Abe does? But to understand music, to play for your own pleasure is wonderful. Believe me, you will thank me one day."

"I'd rather go to dancing school," I sulked, still unconvinced.

"And so you will, next season, with your cousins Rose and May, when Brooks' new term starts. I'll have to make time and go up to Bests' to copy a few of their fancy dresses for dancing school."

I brightened up at the prospect of a few additions to my wardrobe.

"And what is more," Mama smiled at me as if she were communicating sensational news, "some day you'll take elocution lessons! Mrs. Meyers' daughter recited a piece at the last meeting of the Ladies Fuel and Aid Society . . . it was wonderful! Everyone cried. You see now why you have to start early, if you want to accomplish anything in this world?"

When other mothers complained that their children had all they could do just going to school and doing their home-work, Mama would say, "Where there's a will, there's a way."

And Mama practiced what she preached. How surprised I was the first time I saw her taking piano lessons from our teacher! I thought it queer for a grown-up woman to sit and play five finger exercises and count out loud the way I did. She tried to squeeze in fifteen minutes of practicing every night but it became more and more difficult for her to spare even that little time. After two years she gave it up entirely. "My fingers are too stiff from other work. Besides, it's more important for the others to practice." Instead whenever she could, she listened to Abe, whose heavy pounding at the keys, accompanied by a steady roar of the pedal was greatly admired. Or she listened to Harry and Ephie, who were taking violin lessons. It was already decreed that when the others grew up, it would be piano or violin for them also.

Mama made no secret of the fact that she was puzzled

and disturbed by the younger boys. "They're so different from the others," she told one of her friends. "Take Sidney. He can sit looking at a spider or a fly for half an hour! 'What are you staring at?' I asked him. A dreamer. God knows what will become of him! And no clock is safe from Ben. Imagine. You know my black marble clock that used to stand on the dining-room mantel? He took out all the insides!"

"Maybe he'll be an inventor some day," the friend replied consolingly. "The world is *meshugge* (crazy) enough as it is, what is there left to invent?" said mother, as she shrugged her shoulders.

David, the youngest, was the spoiled darling of us all. I was frequently expected to mind him after school, but it was not a very burdensome task, as I usually forgot his presence for hours at a time. In fact he interfered so little with my affairs that once he wandered away and got lost without my having noticed his absence. After hours of distracted search by the family and the whole block, he was brought home by Mike, a big, kindly Irish policeman who had found him near the river, crying with fright but still able to tell where he lived. Mike thereafter became the family's friend, or rather Mama became his, and she showed her gratitude in the tangible shape of gifts of shirts from the shop.

Although she rarely admitted it, there were times when even Mama, the redoubtable, was tired, particularly after a long day at the shop and getting Sidney, Ben and David off to bed. This was often a long drawn-out affair, in which Emma and Papa were occasionally called on for assistance. Papa had only to put his foot on the stair, he rarely needed to go further. The strap, long noodled leather strips attached to a wooden handle, and customary in every house I knew, hung in our kitchen on a nail. Mama, when words failed to make the necessary impression, used it to threaten us with the remark, "If you don't stop, I will call Papa to get the strap." That was usually enough. Papa, we all knew, had a temper and his eyes blazed when he got angry. But we grew to fear his anger more than the strap which he was so frequently expected to wield, but which he never did.

Papa was always tired at night, worn out from his long hours at the shop. After supper, he would sit in the dining-room, his long thin legs stretched out on another chair, his brows knitted over his newspaper, occasionally stroking his short pointed beard, as he studied and worried about the political situation in our city. He took his citizenship seriously and the disclosures of dishonesty hurt him, for he loved America deeply, as only one could who had grown up in Russia, where freedom and liberty were unknown. He would explain things to Mama. He tried to puzzle them out for himself and talk them over with her. "I can't understand it, Fannie, I can't get it through my head. That there was bribery and corruption in Russia was not surprising. With the Czar and his bandits, how else could one live? But here in America, why should there be this graft? We can elect honest people; we vote for the president, the governor, the mayor. What do we need a Tammany Hall for—to put in their bosses and their judges? They make a mockery of every election. The poorest peddler has to hand over graft, even to the police."

But Mama wasn't listening very attentively. Her head was busy with a hundred things as she flitted back and forth from kitchen to dining-room. She stood at the door a few minutes to listen to him, but was more interested in Harry playing the violin than in the shortcomings of Mr. Croker, the Tammany boss. She nodded to Papa to listen too, smiling, content that life should be so good. She was soon back in the kitchen. If it was Thursday night, Emma needed her help to prepare the fish and to set the loaves of *chalas* (Sabbath bread) and pans of yeast cake. If it was a holiday, she would furiously attack some of the closets. No one could satisfy her passion for cleanliness.

In the midst of all this, there sat in the kitchen, night after night, the *lanzmen*, newcomers to America who were sent by Yankele or Rachele, friends of friends from the old country. They would wait uncomplainingly until Mama was at leisure. Mama and Papa, like so many others already rooted in the land of their adoption, helped the bewildered and often penniless newcomers from the old country. In Yiddish and with eloquent gestures they told the stories of their hardships. We children paid little enough attention to the tragedies they often reenacted before our eyes, but unconsciously grasped something of their quiet despair. Yet we could not fail to understand the blessings which, upon leaving, they showered upon our house.

Some of these visitors could be very exasperating. One night a *lanzman* remained after the others had left. As Mama walked back and forth carrying things from the kitchen to the dining-room, he followed her doggedly, intent upon discussing further his own problem.

"What should I do if Claflin refuses to sell me goods?"

"You'll tell him that we'll be responsible for your credit. Wait, to make sure, Mr. L. will go with you. Stop worrying! Listen to my Harry. Tell me, did you ever hear a boy of twelve years play like that?"

The *lanzman* stopped only long enough for an appreciative "Tche, tche, he's a regular genius," and then promptly went right on.

"So I'll have to look for a store right away—and if I find one, who'll sit in the store when I'm out peddling? My wife is *azah kranke* (such a sick one). How can I manage alone?"

Mama, impatient at last, answered the pessimist, "*Sei nicht a pferd* (don't be such a horse). You must try. Nothing ventured, nothing gained. In the end, if it doesn't go, there will always be time to take a job in our shop."

Meanwhile the young genius, undisturbed by talk or argument, continued his practicing. His face was set, his head bent over his bow, his foot tapping out the measures. His eyes, absorbed and dream-like, alone revealed his love for his violin.

My book had been open at the same page for the last half hour, as I continued to mumble to myself the names of explorers of North America. I closed the book in despair. Whatever I secretly thought about the scraping of Harry on his violin, I realized it was beautiful music to Mama and Papa.

3

THE SHOP

MAMA HAD to be away all day in the shop. I could
not imagine what it was my Papa and Mama did there
all day long. The mystery was only partially explained
when Mama took me there one day. I was to remember
it especially, for it was also my first day at school. To
wait at home until ten or eleven o'clock when the school
principal could see Mama, seemed an unconscionable waste
of time. It was simpler to take me along to the shop until
it was time to attend to school enrollment.

The ride on the little horse-car that February morning
was an event. Kneeling on the seat, my face glued to the
window, I watched the driver slacken his reins to let the
horses run, then with a loud whoa, pull them to a standstill to let off a passenger. The horses were spirited and
the bells on their harness tinkled. As they tossed their
heads little clouds of steam rose from their nostrils and
enveloped them in a kind of mist.

All too soon we had to get off. We walked the few

short blocks from Canal Street to Lispenard Street. We entered a dull gray building whose front doors led into a large room filled with men and boys. They were sitting at desks or busily walking up and down, carrying sheaves of paper, pencils stuck jauntily behind their ears.

I tagged after Mama as she made straight for the freight elevator, a huge cavern on which wooden cases were loaded; but we managed somehow to squeeze in.

"Barney, leave us off at the factory floor."

"What's a factory?" I asked Mama. "I thought this was a shop."

"A factory is a place where they manufacture things. You'll see what I mean in a few minutes."

Barney smiled. "Already she wants to know about business!" I looked up at the big burly figure, his horny hands grasping the iron cables as we crept up the shaft. "So you don't remember me," the thickened hoarse voice continued. "I came from Russia with your Papa. Many a glass of tea I had in your house. Now you won't forget me, Sophele."

The factory was on the third floor. Girls were sitting at machines working on yards of white goods trimmed with embroidery. Mama examined some of the finished work. There were ladies' nightgowns with long sleeves, drawers made nice and full with a drawstring of tape for the waist; and petticoats with deep ruffles, wide and stiff so as to make the dresses stick out in what was then the fashion. Mama had a smile and a pleasant word for everyone and you could see they did not think of her as just the "boss." Soon she was deep in work, going over papers with Dave, her bookkeeper, but she noticed out of the corner of her eye that the girls were still talking and fussing with me and she called to me to "stop bothering everybody."

I walked away. I wanted to see what the rest of the floor was like. There were shelves right up to the ceiling, filled with white goods, and with little ladders conveniently placed for reaching them. I climbed up to the top of one of the ladders where I could see and hear everything. Mama seemed to be talking to everyone at once. "No, I won't give you another order, your threads keep on breaking. No, my word is final; even a child does not wait to get burned twice. Dave, call downstairs and find out how many gross buttons we need. And find out from the shipping department what happened to that order for Chicago."

Mama left the office. Only Dave, the bookkeeper, remained. An office meant pencils and paper. I got down the ladder and pushed open the glass partition door. "Dave—can I sit on one of these stools, too?"

Soon I was busy collecting enough pencils, pens, rubber bands and blotters to supply our whole block. It wasn't long before I clambered down again, and I was soon wandering around, looking for a safe place to deposit my booty. I decided to explore another part of the loft building and climbed the tall stairs that led to the next floor. As I stood on the top step, I could hear Papa arguing with a man who was bent over the table, cutting cloth with a sharp knife, guided by a pattern.

I had never seen such long tables; they stretched the whole length of the loft and the striped dark material spread out upon them looked like a long unrolled carpet.

The men wore short dark blue aprons tied around their waists and were carefully cutting designs into the cloth. Everyone seemed quiet and busy, except Papa, who was saying to one of them in a loud and angry voice, "Bandit, you spoiled the whole lot, and now they're only good for seconds!" Whatever that meant, it made Papa angrier than ever.

No one noticed me, so I was glad to go down again to the floor below, with its buzz and hum of the machines and some of the girls singing snatches of song. Mama was now sitting at a machine too, her feet going like lightning, ruffling yards and yards of embroidery which cascaded into an immense box, already almost overflowing. "Mrs. L., Mrs. L.," voices were calling, and Mama left her machine.

I was tired, I had explored everything. I climbed on Mama's chair, slid easily into the case and crawled under the mountain of ruffles until I felt the hard, smooth boards. I stretched out and closed my eyes. I became the heroine of my fancy and my eyes grew wet in self-pity! The snow was falling, I was completely covered with it; nothing to keep me warm but one little match—I was the poor little match-girl, freezing to death in the snow.

I heard my name called, but it was pleasant lying under the ruffles, their prickly edges stinging me. The biting snow became even more real. Again I heard my name. There was no mistaking it that time. Someone was frightened. I stood up, my head barely emerging, entangled in a mass of twisted ruffles. There was a cry from the girl nearest me, "Here she is, Mrs. L.," as she lifted me out of the case. "Your Mama thought you fell down the elevator!" There was Mama still peering down the yawning depths of the freight elevator shaft; it was her agonized call I had heard. Mama said little as she came over to me, fixed my crumpled dress and combed my hair, but I could tell from her face that she felt the factory was no place for me. Arthur, one of the young men who, though only seventeen, was already a budding salesman whom Mama admired because of the beautiful way he spoke English, was summoned and duly instructed to take me to school.

Arthur took me as far as the class room and was now saying goodbye. "Please, please, don't go away," I begged. But neither entreaty nor tears were of avail— Arthur had to go back to the shop. With beating heart I took the seat in the back of the room which the teacher had indicated with her long sharp pointer.

That night in bed, with little David fast asleep next to me, his long golden curls a crumpled mass around his face, I recounted to the two younger brothers lying wide-eyed in the bed next to my own, not only the wonder of the first day of school but all about what I had seen in the shop.

"Do you know what they make on the top floor of the loft, on tables as long as this whole block, with goods on them that stretch as far as you can see? Shirts, like Abe and Harry wear every day, and nightgowns just like Papa wears when he goes to bed."

It was many years before I visited the shop again, a self-conscious adolescent. The sewing machines and the long line of girls sitting at them had long disappeared. Not only was the building changed to a better one, but the work on the top floor had now invaded the other floors as well. Men of all ages were pressing shirts with large irons, the steam filling the air. Boys were folding, pinning and packing them into the boxes that later went into the cases that I remembered having crowded me in the freight elevator years ago. Only Dave, the bookkeeper, seemed unchanged, looking just as youthful as ever as he pored over the books, sitting on a tall stool at his private desk. Girls only a few years older than I were competently taking dictation and were eyeing me curiously out of the corner of their eyes. I felt lonely. I missed the warm intimacy of the earlier day. As I stood there, shy and awkward, I hoped they would not dislike me because I was the boss's daughter.

4

THE THREE R'S

READING, Writing, and 'Rithmetic were the staples of instruction in the public schools of New York City fifty years ago—these and "deportment." When teacher called out in her sharp, penetrating voice, "Class!" everyone sat up straight as a ramrod, eyes front, hands clasped rigidly behind one's back. We strived painfully to please her. With a thin smile of approval on her face, her eyes roved over the stiff, rigid figures in front of her.

Beautiful script letters across the huge blackboard and a chart of the alphabet were the sole adornments of the classroom. Every day the current lesson from our speller was meticulously written out on the blackboard by the teacher who, whatever else she lacked, wrote a lovely, regular hand. We spent hours over our copybooks, all conveniently lined, as we laboriously sought to imitate this perfection.

We had to learn our lessons by heart, and we repeated them out loud until we memorized them. Playgrounds were non-existent, toilets were in the yard, and gymnasiums were an unheard of luxury. In the fifth and sixth grades, we had a few minutes for "exercise." At the command, "Class stand!" our ears were shattered by the shuffling of fifty pairs of feet and the banging of noisily raised seats. The window was opened a fraction of an inch and the teacher, standing on her little platform beside her desk, snapped, "Breathe in! . . . Breathe out!" The hissing sounds as we "exhaled" must have reminded the teacher of a school of porpoises at play. Now that our lungs were bursting with oxygen, we proceeded to real "exercise."

"Hands on shoulders, arms up, arms out, shoulders back . . . arms up, arms out!"

After five minutes of this, the class, just beginning to show unmistakable signs of getting out of hand, was ordered to "sit," and the teacher sank exhausted in her seat.

I was an earnest pupil, always eager to do well. But no amount of diligence could overcome my inability to grasp arithmetic. One day I heard, "Sophie, come to my desk." I walked uncertainly, wondering what I had done wrong. We had just finished our sewing period, an hour we all liked, as it permitted us some relaxation from our usual discipline. We did not make useful things, dresses or aprons, as they do in school today, but did samples of stitches, basting and tiny running stitches, backstitches and hemming, all in scarlet thread on little white muslin squares. Only partially reassured by the teacher's smile, I faced the class, shy and self-conscious.

"This is her sewing," my teacher said. I looked up despondently at my sampler dangling in the teacher's fingers, but she continued sweetly, "It is a perfect example of neat and regular sewing. Now you may read your composition to the class. It is very good," and she handed me my paper from the pile on her desk.

I don't remember exactly what the composition was about, but I have a dim recollection that it concerned a poor little immigrant girl whose parents had died at sea while coming to America. Hungry and friendless, she roamed the streets. I remembered the hardships of the newcomers to America who had sat so patiently in Mama's kitchen and so I invested my little immigrant girl in the composition I wrote for school with the pathos of the actual stories I had heard. Tears filled my eyes as I finished, and the girls in the class looked sad. I sniffed as I tried to reach for the handkerchief lost in the deep pocket of my dress.

The teacher was speaking again. As in a dream, I heard her say, "Now, Sophie, because you did so nicely, you may be monitor for the arithmetic period. Copy on the blackboard the problems you had for homework and you may explain them to the class, for I must say that only you and a few others got the correct answers."

My hands shook and the chalk stuck to my fingers as I began to write on the blackboard about a barrel of potatoes some grocer wanted to divide into bushels and pecks and quarts. I now held the teacher's long pointer and turned to the class. I wet my lips and tried to begin. I shook my head.

"Take the next problem," said the teacher in an effort to help me.

But I was no happier with gallons of milk which the

farmer wanted to separate into quarts, pints and gills. Miserably I again shook my head. The teacher was displeased. She had counted on me. I had failed her and the class was snickering.

"But you handed in a perfect paper. What is the trouble?" she asked. I blurted out that my big brother Harry had helped me do them.

"And how about the composition, did big brother Harry do that, too?" At my vehement protests of "No, No," the class only laughed.

I got to my seat somehow. I thought sadly to myself that there would be no need now for Lizzie to prick me with a pin or to tug slyly at my hair to make me jump and break that bolt upright posture which teacher expected of us. "No," I thought bitterly, "now she will leave me alone, for I am no longer the teacher's pet."

5

THE DENTIST

MY FIRST VISIT to a dentist was when I was about seven years old. I had a toothache and it seriously interfered with my eating lemon cocoanut taffy, a delicacy I adored, as well as with more substantial food. Mama marched me off to the dentist. His office was on Grand Street, and a tremendous gold tooth swayed from his window under an equally huge sign which announced, "Painless Dentistry."

Mama carefully explained to me, "Pulling out a tooth only a few years ago was something terrible—today, it's a pleasure. You don't feel a thing, that's what the sign means."

We entered the waiting room. Frightened by the strong smell of something unpleasant as well as the deep groans emerging from behind the closed office door, I was, despite Mama's reassuring words, all for running home at once. Mama only pressed me more firmly into my seat. She had stayed home from business specially, it had been a job to get me there, and she had no intention of letting me escape. The groans continued and after what seemed hours, the patient came out and I went in and sat down in the chair just vacated.

While I was still investigating the wheel and the other gadgets that stood next to me, the chair fell back and I with it, my feet rising in the air.

"Open your mouth wide," the dentist ordered sweetly. I felt his breath as he poked something in my mouth, his spectacled face next to mine. "Now, little girl," he said, trying to make his voice sugary, "which is the one that is giving you all that trouble?" I was about to reply, but all I could manage were gurgling noises. Before I could think what one did in this strange circumstance, I saw a flash of a large and terrifying instrument entering my mouth. Then followed a crunching tug and yank, and suddenly the dentist was cheerfully exhibiting my tooth. While I sat up and rinsed my mouth, he was neatly wrapping it up for me to take home as a trophy. I now howled in earnest, more out of anger and fright than pain; only the shiny silver quarter that my Mama gave me induced me to stop my racket.

You couldn't help knowing in those days when anyone had a toothache. It was quite the usual thing to see girls come to school, their swollen cheeks wrapped in a wool stocking fastened with a large safety pin, or in a large colored handkerchief. When this treatment failed to cure, the tooth was invariably pulled. Filling teeth was considered a waste of time and money.

I remember our Emma going about for days with her cheek swollen to the size of a pumpkin, her face swathed in red flannel smeared with grease, a remedy she had brought from the old country. When after a few days, that didn't help, she put a bag of hot salt under the kerchief, like a poultice. We youngsters used to laugh—she looked so funny with one slit of an eye peeping out of that poor moon-like face. Mama got her to go to the dentist at last and she returned minus a dozen teeth. It was pretty discouraging for Emma to have great gaps in her mouth. Soon she had the rest of her teeth pulled, and shortly thereafter she received a set of brand new ones, which had been the dentist's idea from the beginning. And so Emma was happy—she would never again get a toothache. Thereafter, upon the slightest encouragement, she would dislodge her plate with a deft twist of her hands, exhibit them admiringly, and pop them back again. They became her most prized possession.

6

THE STREET

WOMEN WORE their skirts down to the ground. That was the fashion, long skirts everyday, no matter what work they did, whether sweeping the sidewalk or scrubbing the floors. When crossing the street, women gathered a handful of their wide skirts to one side, and discreetly lifted them, careful not to expose even an ankle to the curious gaze of a male passer-by.

Often we watched Mama walking down the street, her skirts blowing and swishing around her feet. Mama, always practical, sewed a little fold of cloth around the bottom, "to catch the dust," she explained, and to save the hem from getting worn. Today we smile incredulously as we think of all the germs that were invited to settle on skirts and dresses as they bobbed up and down the sidewalk. If there was peril from the microbes breeding in the dust, or from the continual droppings of the horses, or from the huge piles of snow shoveled into great heaps and then left forgotten to blacken until it thawed and disappeared, we were happily unaware of it.

Children owned the streets in a way unthinkable to city children of today. There were a few parks, but too distant to be of any use, and so the street was the common playground. The separation of boys and girls so rigidly carried out in the public school also held on the street; boys played with boys, girls with girls. Occasionally we girls might stand on the sidelines and watch the boys play their games, but usually our presence was ignored. There was no doubt about it, girls were considered inferior creatures. The athletic girl, the girl who would fearlessly decide on a career or even demand the right to study a profession, was still unknown. Teaching alone was grudgingly admitted as being "respectable" for a girl. Going to College was the rare achievement for a few hardy souls, but for most, it was only a dream. We knew it to be a boy's world, but we didn't seem to mind it too much. We shared the life of the street unhampered by our parents who were too busy to try to mold us into a more respectable pattern. If we lacked the close supervision of the genteel world of maids and governesses, we gloried all the more in our freedom from restriction.

All the really colorful street events were taken over by the boys, on Halloween, July 4th and especially on Election night. For weeks before Election Day, self-styled orators, standing on wagons lit up by flares, harangued groups of people on street corners, describing with gusto the superlative merits of their respective candidates. The Republican spokesman shouted his denunciation of his opponent, while the Democrat at the next corner returned

the insults with interest. Then a new kind of speechmaker made his appearance, one spoken of with contempt by the other two contenders—the Socialist. "Sure," someone would heckle from the crowd, "promise them everything, promises are cheap, but it'll be the same old song and dance when *you* get into office." "Get in?" still another jeered, "Why, he hasn't a Chinaman's chance!" Undisturbed by horse-laughs and witticisms, the speaker went on, talking quietly, persuasively, of the low wages, the long hours and the bosses who "grind out the labor of their brothers in filthy sweatshops."

Much of this we heard discussed at home as well as by the cart-tail orators. It was in the air we breathed, and although we were either ardent Republicans, or else unregenerate Democrats, we were united in a common dislike of the "new messiah," the Socialist candidate who was preaching discontent to the working man. My father, like all the business men of his day, shrugged his shoulders at these "crackpots" and "agitators." "Are we not all workers?" he said. "Are my hours of labor less than theirs? Don't they earn more money here in America than they ever dreamed would be theirs?"

We children would listen in bored silence. On Election Day our interest would suddenly revive. For days, the boys on our block had been collecting wood, taken from unfinished buildings; grocers had been made to disgorge boxes and barrels. This treasure, which had been carefully stowed away, was now piled high on the curb. Election Night meant only one thing to us: our bonfire had to be bigger and better than the one on the next block. As the fire blazed, boys threw potatoes into the embers and later ate them with loud relish, their faces smeared with the blackened mickies. The crowning glory of Election Night was the triumphant parade of the victorious party. The band played, slogans and banners floated in the wind, and brooms were held high to announce with derision the clean sweep of victory.

All my pleading to stay up and watch the parade to the end, was fruitless. My brother Ephie, reinforced by the commands of Mama and Papa, virtually would have to drag me away.

Except on such rare occasions, we girls played only girls' games. Tagging after us sometimes were our little brothers and sisters whom we were supposed to mind, but that was no great hardship or hindrance. We would toss them our bean-bags, little cloth containers filled with cherry pits. "Now see that you play here on the stoop or you won't get any ice cream when the hoky-poky man comes along." The hope of getting that penny's worth of ice cream dished out on a bit of brown paper, was sufficient to quell any incipient revolt on the part of our little charges. Thus unhampered, we could proceed to our game of potsy. Mama didn't like me to play potsy. She thought it "disgraceful" to mark up our sidewalk with chalk for our lines and boxes; besides, hopping on one foot and pushing the thick piece of tin, I managed to wear out a pair of shoes in a few weeks! I obeyed her wishes in my own way, by playing farther down the street and marking up someone else's sidewalk.

Neither my friends nor I played much with dolls. Since families generally had at least one baby on hand, we girls had plenty of opportunity to shower upon the baby broth-

ers or sisters the tenderness and love that would otherwise
have been diverted to dolls. Besides, dolls were expensive.
We often stopped to look at the shop windows on Grand
Street. The dolls were gorgeous: blue-eyed bits of perfection dressed in unimaginable splendor. Next to them, as
if ready for a journey, were miniature trunks filled with
clothes, from tiny white leather shoes to poke bonnet.
What else could one do with such a doll except look at it
in ecstatic wonder?

Regardless of season, the favorite game of both boys
and girls was "prisoner's base." We lined up on opposite
sides of the curb, our numbers evenly divided, represent-
ing two enemy camps. One side turned its back to invite
a surprise attack. Stealthily a contestant advanced and
either safely reached the "enemy" and captured a "prisoner," or, if caught, became a "prisoner." Shouts of de-
fiance could be heard a block off when someone was captured. When a sufficient number of prisoners had been
taken, a tug of war followed to rescue them. Trucks and
brewery wagons lumbered by. We looked upon them
merely as an unnecessary interference with the progress
of our game. Sometimes, to be sure, accidents occurred,
but they were rare; either we were very fleet of foot or
the drivers obligingly slowed their horses.

One little incident remains obstinately with me. We
were all set to play "prisoner's base," but needed one more
girl to make an even number on each side. Just then
Miriam came along. She held back, said she didn't want to
play. She had on a new dress, but we didn't pay any attention to that. I didn't realize until later that it was the
dress she was supposed to wear only on the Sabbath day,

and that she had begged to wear it to school to show it to
her teacher. I called to her, "Come on, don't be a scare-
cat!" Unable to resist our coaxing, she took her place in
the line. At the very end of the game she was lined up
against me. We were evenly matched, and we each stood
our ground, feet firmly planted on the cobblestone, right
hands clasped as we pulled and strained. Neither of us
would give way. Suddenly I heard the horse car and the
angry clang of the bell. Something would have to be done,
or the game would be spoiled. I clenched my teeth. With
one desperate pull I dragged Miriam to my side, and as
she rolled on the muddy stones I felt the joy of victory.
But at what a cost! That dress, so neat and pretty a short
while ago, was unrecognizable, and there was a tear right
down the middle. After the others left, Miriam sadly admitted to me she was afraid to go home. Would I go with
her? Soberly we mounted the three flights of stairs. There
in the dimness of the kitchen was Mrs. Klein, Miriam's
mother, ironing the school dress Miriam would wear the
next day. I recognized it, for Miriam had only two
dresses. Mrs. Klein smiled when she saw me, and then she
noticed Miriam. I still shiver as I recall the anger and
terror of her words.

"*Schtick mist*, good-for-nothing, waster—to spoil and
ruin your only good dress. Where," asked Mrs. Klein as
she tearfully wrung her hands, "where am I, a widow,
working my fingers to the bone, to get the money to buy
another one, and the holidays only a few weeks off!"

I pleaded for Miriam, said over and over again it was
my fault. I dared not say that I would ask my Mama to

make good the dress, as if it were no more than a pane of glass I had broken.

"Go, take off the dress," Mrs. Klein said finally. "I will try to fix it." She sat in her chair, staring ahead of her. "In the end, it is only a dress, and children must play. God forbid, she could have been hurt."

I saw with relief that her anger was over, and I got up to leave. She kept on talking, as if to herself, "A torn dress can be mended, a broken life is a different matter. Downstairs, on the second floor, at Mrs. Cohen's, they have real *tzores* (trouble). Their little girl, *uf nicht uns gesagt* (may it not happen to us). . . ." she sighed. Then she turned solemnly to us as we stood in the doorway. "Don't either of you ever go near that cursed shoemaker in the cellar next door. May he soon *lieg in dred* (lie in his grave). But I'm forgetting—your Mama will be worried. It is time for you to go, my child."

Yes, the street gave us our friends. It was the playground where we met, fought, danced, dreamed. It taught us more than we realized, at the time, for it made us aware, if dimly, of the life, both good and evil, that was unfolding about us.

7

PAPA AND MAMA GO OUT

MAMA WORKED long hours in the shop, and when she got home she was often busy late into the night. All in the house would be ready for bed, and we would see her, still sitting at her machine, mending sheets or tablecloths or turning out another "fancy dress" for me, copied, as usual, from some fabulous shop uptown. She had so much vitality, such enormous energy, that nothing seemed to tire her, not the long day, nor her worry for us with our inevitable procession of scarlet fever, diphtheria, chicken pox, or measles. Mama also loved a good time and was ready for one at the drop of a hat.

Every spring there was a Strawberry Festival. Of course, strawberries were served as refreshment, but the chief attraction was the variety show that had been planned months in advance and was to be the theme of reminiscent delight for months after. We used to repeat the jokes of the Irish or German comedians, warble a garbled version of a few strains of *La Bohème* with which the opera singer had favored us, and would try some of the baffling tricks of the magician. We children were often taken along because the additional sale of tickets helped to swell the funds, and mothers felt more at ease with their offspring under their eyes. Although everyone had a grand time, these affairs, were primarily given to raise money. Perhaps it was for the Beth Israel Hospital that had just opened its doors on the Lower East Side, or to provide coal for the freezing tenants in the dark and evil-looking tenements. The concern which Jews always felt about their poor dates back to the early Jewish settlers in the days of Peter Stuyvesant. They overcame his unfriendliness and unwillingness for them to settle in New Amsterdam, by promising to look after their own destitute, a pledge that has never been forgotten.

An Annual Ball provided additional funds to help take care of the needy. It was "the Ball" of the Ladies Fuel and Aid Society, the big social event of the winter, held at Madison Square Garden. For months tickets were sold and donations solicited. Dressmakers worked day and night turning out new dresses or cleverly disguising old ones. Every gown had a train which majestically swept the floor. Busts were large, hips were generous, and the bodices heavily boned and smartly drawn in at the waist line to give that fulsome, rounded look so ardently admired by Mama and all the ladies.

Mama was dressing for the affair and was being laced up in her corset by Mary, lately added to our household to relieve Emma. "What's the matter with you, Mary? Pull the laces tighter, don't be afraid." Mama then continued her interrupted conversation with Papa through

the plush portieres. Thus far he had remained unmoved by her insistent reminder, "it's getting late. Why don't you dress?" But now he had reached the apologetic stage. "Take one of the children," he mildly suggested. "What should I do at a ball?" I was playing with Mama's rings that lay on the bureau. They had just been cleaned and were sparkling for the great occasion. I was wondering how Mama was going to get around Papa . . . perhaps I would be taken after all!

Slipping into a petticoat, Mama began again, tactfully changing the subject. "You know, Simon, I have a feeling that ladies' muslin underwear will soon be behind the times. I hear that in Paris women are wearing pants, regular men's pants. . . . Mary, hand me the other petticoat, the one with the lace flounce. I tell you, Simon, no sensible woman is going to keep wearing these white embroidery drawers and petticoats that take a girl half a day to iron. And at the wages we have to pay today! I don't mean you, Mary, I'm glad to pay *you* the sixteen dollars a month, you at least are worth it, but some of these greenhorns. . . . I'm telling you, Simon, muslin underwear will soon be a back number."

Papa was interested; he forgot he was tired. "And what do you propose?" he asked. "How can you make a living from shirts alone, when today every shoemaker considers himself a shirt manufacturer? Look at the competition we have."

Mama carefully put her dress on over her head, so as not to disturb the elaborate coiffure painstakingly arranged by the hairdresser. "Yes," she continued, as she critically examined herself in the mirror, "competitors in

making cheap shirts we have plenty, but to make something new!" Mary was now bent double, hooking up the
dress, squinting at the dozens of invisible little hooks
and eyes that went down the back to below the waist. "I
got an idea last night, Simon. I couldn't sleep for thinking of it. I would like to see us make a shirt with the
collar and cuffs attached. Why should a man always have
to hunt for his collar and cuffs? They should be sewn
right onto the shirt itself. I tell you, it can be a big
thing! Sophie, go look at the clock and tell me what
time it is. Eight o'clock! And you sit there, Simon, like
a block of wood. I ask you, how can the Treasurer of the
Society go to the Ball without her husband? No, there's
no time now to talk about this idea of mine, but it's all in
my head. Come, get dressed. Your suit and things are
lying here all ready on the bed. We'll talk about it when
we ride uptown." And so Papa went to the ball.

When Mama got dressed up, we children looked upon
her with new eyes. In her long, black velvet dress, her
white shoulders gleaming, a necklace of shining stones
at her throat, her black, wavy hair piled high on her
head, Mama was handsome and young!

Papa went to these affairs only after Mama bullied him
into going. He went glum and unhappy, but Mama knew
that once there, he would discover old friends and enjoy
himself. And judging by his comment the following day,
"It wasn't so bad," he no doubt *had* enjoyed himself.

But going to the theater was Mama's most regular
and satisfying form of having a good time. We knew
many of the actors. They were not people removed from
us in their experience or outlook, but folks like ourselves,

only gifted with that wonderful power to evoke tears or laughter. One famous comedian lived right next door, a man excruciatingly funny on the stage, yet always morose at home. His wife was a frequent visitor at our house, whispering to Mama, with ever-ready tears, about her husband's "carryings-on." Mama's wrath would smolder and finally explode at the recital of such unfaithfulness, only to subside quickly with a meaningful nod in my direction, "Better *she* shouldn't hear about such things."

At least one evening every week Mama would say, "Well, Simon, will you go to the show?" Papa would inquire, "Is it a comedy?" "No, I think it is a drama; they say Tomashefsky has a wonderful part." "Tomashefsky," Papa would retort, "a tragedy, I suppose. I see and hear enough *tzores* (woes) every day. Besides, how can I get up at six o'clock in the morning if I go to bed at all hours? But if you want to go . . . go . . . take one of the children."

We all began in a chorus, "Mama, can I go?" How Mama ever decided whom to take, I'll never know, but it seemed no matter who else went, I, too, managed to go along. We did not go to the English-speaking theatre uptown on Fourteenth Street. We were bound for the Yiddish theater, the Thalia, or the Windsor, where Jewish playwrights wrote for Jewish actors and Jewish audiences. But the audience was not entirely Jewish. Theatrical producers from Broadway and professors of literature at Columbia University were beginning to come to the Yiddish theatres to see for themselves the plays and the acting that were already the talk of New York.

The Yiddish theater on the East Side was flourishing.

Great actors from Europe were glad to perform before
such an admiring and appreciative audience. Like the
Synagogue and the Annual Ball, the theater served as a
social function. There was no reserve among the audience,
everyone talked to everyone else. During the intermission
it was a common sight to see some well-cushioned ladies
standing in the orchestra aisle waving their arms or
making sounds like "pst, pst," to attract the attention
of friends in the gallery and converse across the vast
expanse of the theater. "How's Mama's feet?" or "Did
you hear who died last week?" There would be voluble
"tut-tuts" and sympathetic wagging of heads. Those who
were near listened with undisguised interest, except when
too busy talking among themselves. Others sociably and
noisily drank soda water purchased from the ushers who
marched up and down the aisles, shrilly calling, "Candy,
soda water, candy, soda water!"

Some of the plays were classics, such as *The Kreutzer
Sonata, Gott, Mench und Teufel,* (God, Man and the
Devil), and works by Shakespeare. I remember a Shylock,
played by the great tragedian, Jacob Adler, who gave
me an unforgettable memory of that great rôle. Some
years later, Adler played it on Broadway, in Yiddish,
with an entire English-speaking cast. Adler was not the
only great star of the Yiddish stage. There were still
others like Madame Kalish, who, speaking both languages
fluently, became an English-speaking star, after her
success on the Yiddish stage. Although enormously
successful on her tour through the States, she came back
time and again to the audiences of the East Side, playing

again before "her *Yiddishe volk*" the roles which she had created.

But it was the simple drama of our own day which I preferred. To me, all plays were good, even the bad ones. Not understanding Yiddish too well, except for occasional words and the homely expressions which embroidered everyone's speech, I relied almost entirely upon the acting, which was so natural and expressive, I could grasp the meaning of the play.

There was one play which served as a pattern for many others. It was the story of a family that had come to America. The son, after a few years, had grown prosperous. He had discarded his religious practices as old-fashioned, and was embarrassed when his aged parents visited his now ultra-fashionable home. He felt he did his duty by providing for their material needs, but this, the father told him, had now become "gall and wormwood in their mouths."

In a scene bordering on the tragic, the mother, in ritual wig, dressed in old-world grandeur, tries in vain to ingratiate herself with her American-born daughter-in-law and her grandchildren. They look upon her as someone strange and alien. The father succeeds no better. He reminds his son, "Your Milton is past eleven years; it is time he was learning for *Bar Mitzvah*."

"Please, father, spare me that," says the son, as he looks uncomfortably at his friends, who are at a table playing pinochle and are highly amused by such a suggestion.

Broken-hearted, the father dies. The grave yawns right before the audience; nothing is left to the imagination.

"I repent, I repent," says the son, as he tries to fling himself into the grave.

The aged mother restrains him, and there follows a tearful reconciliation. "You can perform a *mitzvah* (good deed) that will bring joy to your father in Paradise," she says. "Your great uncle's only child is an old maid; already she is twenty. If you, my son, will provide the wedding and the dowry for this penniless orphan, a husband can be found."

With the assistance of the *shadchan* (marriage broker), a comic but nostalgic figure to those who so recently came from Europe, but an object of ridicule to the American-born children, the match is made. The *chuppa* (wedding canopy) is brought on the stage, and after a ceremony in which tears flow freely, there are feasting and rejoicing. The *shammus* (sexton), his red bandana streaming from his coat-tails, starts a traditional dance in which the male guests solemnly join. Women stand in a circle and clap their hands as they beat out the rhythm. The music grows wilder and wilder. The curtain falls.

To Mama and to us it was all simply wonderful.

We made our way into the street and hurried home, Mama anxiously aware of the lateness of the hour. But I remained under the spell of the theater until I fell asleep.

8

HAVE YOU HEARD?

JUST AS PAPA could rarely be induced to go to a ball or the theater, he was equally obdurate on the question of paying visits to relatives or friends. "If they are so anxious to see us," he would tell Mama, "let them come here." Although his scowl looked forbidding at the news of such an impending visit, he was gracious enough when the visitors came, and he remained pleasant and smiling all through the evening, unless, of course, they stayed too late.

He had less patience for the neighbors who dropped in "just for a few moments." "Sit down, sit down," Mama hospitably urged. In a flash she took the large pressed glass fruit bowl from the sideboard, filled it with fruit, set tiers of raisins on the top, and then, as a last touch, stuck in the five or six pearl-handled fruit knives at appropriate angles. The inevitable glasses of tea soon followed. The visitors sat at the table, but they seemed more intent on preserving the unbroken spirals of the orange rind or apple skin they were peeling than in their casual chatter, or what Papa later called *shmoos* (gossip). I was forgotten in my corner.

"Have you heard? Mendel's daughter is going with that good-for-nothing son of Noah Roth. I grant you, the father is an upright man, but has he ever known how to control his son? No! They say he even goes with actresses and gambles. If it were my daughter he were courting he would never cross our threshold. I told Mendel myself, 'The girl has lots of time. America is not Poland. Here a girl is not considered an old maid until she is at least twenty. What is the hurry?' Do you know what he answered me? 'She loves him!' Did you ever hear such *stuss* (nonsense)? And where will all that love business be when he leaves her, maybe with a half a dozen children, and runs off with an actress? A leopard never changes his spots. Believe me, he will bring Noah Roth to an untimely grave." Our visitor bit the piece of sugar she had held poised in her hand, took a deep gulp of the scalding tea, wrathfully shook her head, and seemed to enjoy her gloomy prophecy.

A friend of Papa's, who had once been a *melamed* (teacher), but now flitted from one occupation to another in his attempt to become a businessman, interrupted with a deep sigh. "Some people have all the luck! Imagine, in Poland, Samuel Yarmelke was so poor and wretched, my mother, of blessed memory, would take pity on him and feed him. Now he is become so prosperous that his tin business is no longer good enough for him. So he is going into the banking business." To the incredulous exclamations of his listeners, he gently replied, "Believe me, I am not dreaming. What is more, he is to open a branch right here on Grand Street. I had it from him myself. 'Poor people need a bank more than rich ones,' he said. I asked him if he were becoming a philanthropist. 'Not entirely,' he laughed, 'but this kind of philanthropy puts money in your pocket, instead of taking it out!' "

Mr. Raphael sighed again, "You see, some people have all the luck, and some, nothing but ill luck. Take my brother-in-law. Out of sheer kindness, he put his signature to a note for a friend, and now he is bankrupt, and the friend whom he thought to save, is also bankrupt. Luck, all you need in the world is luck!"

Mrs. Wolkowitz, the tenant from the top floor, was eating raisins and cautiously spitting the seeds into her plate. "Since I've got these gold crowns on my teeth, I can eat anything," she confided to Mama. "How do you like them?"

Mama looked and nodded her approval. "They seem good and strong, only it is a pity they have to be your front teeth."

"Why is it a pity?" Mrs. Wolkowitz asked indignantly. "Believe me, the fortune it cost me, it should be in the front. Besides, I think they are very becoming."

Mama's answer was lost in the excitement of the fire engines passing our house, their bells clanging, the beat of the galloping horses plainly heard. "Tch, tch," Mrs. Wolkowitz shook her head, "that's the third fire tonight right in this neighborhood! Poor Sam Levine had a fire in his store last week. Jake says it was lucky that it was the end of the season, otherwise it would have been a real misfortune."

Papa growled at her. "A fire is always a misfortune."

The dining-room clock struck nine, and the guests hurriedly reminded themselves that they must be going. Mama did nothing to dissuade them, and soon they *were* gone. When the door closed on the last of them, Papa took up his neglected newspaper, muttering, "Idle tongues and empty heads—the men as bad as the women!"

Neither my friends nor I shared Papa's disdain for idle talk, and we had our own ideas of the social amenities. Seated as usual on the stoop, munching with relish a sour vinegar pickle, purchased from the German delicatessen store around the corner, we regaled each other with incidents of our own experience, often embellished in the retelling.

"Chinamen eat mice, you know that, don't you?" We listened to Miriam as she unfolded her latest revelation about these strange people. A Chinese laundryman had his little shop only a few blocks away, and he seemed to us mysterious and frightening. We often looked at him, as he bent over his iron while we warily passed his doorway. His yellow skin, shorn head, and queue, which was dangling far below his waist, filled us with terror. We were ready to believe anything.

"My brother," Miriam continued, "asked me to call for his shirts, and I told him I wouldn't. I would be scared to go into the Chinkie's place!"

"What did he say to that?" we asked.

"He told me not to be a fool." She shrugged her

shoulders. "Oh, and he said a lot about their being such a wonderful people, that they had poets and writers before other people."

" 'If they're so wonderful,' I answered him, 'why do they eat mice?' 'They don't,' he answered me. 'How do you know they don't—the Lillifels say they do, and they ought to know; their store is right next to the laundry.' 'Oh, forget it!' he said. 'Will you just stop in at Charlie Lee's and ask him for my shirts?' "

"Did you go?" we asked in one breath.

"No, I just wouldn't."

We were relieved. Prejudices were comfortable, made us feel important, superior to others, and we wouldn't relinquish ours without a struggle.

Lizzie broke in, anxiously waiting for her chance to get in a word. "Have you heard that my cousin Jack was in another fight and had to have his lip sewed up in the hospital?"

"No! How did it happen?"

"Well, he was playing One O'Cat on Montgomery Street, near Murphy's Saloon. One of the boys gave the stick such a whack that it went right through the door of the saloon. Jack tried to catch it, just as a big fellow came through the swinging door carrying a can of beer. He stumbled and yelled, 'What are you trying to do, you sheeny, trip me up?' Jack got up and yelled right back, 'What are you trying to do, you big Mick, drown me in your beer?' The next thing you knew, they were both fighting, and the people from the saloon and on the sidewalk egged them on, taking sides. By the time they were separated, they were both bleeding something terrible. The big man shook his fist at Jack, saying, 'I'm not through with you yet, wait till I get my gang after you.' "

We mournfully shook our heads. We already envisaged Jack in their toils!

"Why can't someone stop these gangs? My Mama is so worried."

"Tell your Mama not to worry anymore," I reassured her. "My Mama and Papa and Mr. and Mrs. Reiss, who live in our house, are getting the neighbors together, all because of these gangs and peddlers and the police."

"What do you mean?" they asked.

"Well, a few days ago Mrs. Reiss was buying some fish in the market on Ludlow Street, when she heard a commotion. A gang was rushing through the street, bullying the peddlers and helping themselves to whatever they wanted. One of the peddlers tried to stop them. They kicked over his pushcart, and all his oranges and lemons rolled away down the muddy street, into the gutters, everywhere. The peddler started screaming, 'Police! Police!' Mrs. Reiss heard the racket and rushed out of the store. She tried to hold one of the loafers until a policeman came, but he threw her down and got away with the others. When the policeman did come, he arrested the peddler for disorderly conduct, for causing a disturbance, he said.

"That night Papa and Mama and Mr. and Mrs. Reiss were boiling mad and they went to the police station to complain. The captain told them to mind their own business Papa answered right back that this was his business, the peddler had been robbed, and the policeman had arrested him instead of going after the gang.

"Mr. Reiss spoke up, too. 'These gangs threaten our storekeepers. They say they will break their windows if they don't hand over money each week.'

"The captain said, 'Sure, it's a shame, but it isn't up to me. I takes my orders from the higher-ups.'

"That settled it. Papa and Mr. Reiss got a lawyer, and they are going to get people from uptown to help them form a Citizens Committee. They're going to wake people up and put a stop to all the gangs."

Our faith in the sure triumph of justice received quite a jolt some weeks later, when, in spite of the lawyer, the case was thrown out of court, and the peddler fined. But, in time, after several years, a Citizens Union did become a reality and was responsible for far-reaching reforms.

It was getting late. Sitting there on the stoop, we could hear the voices calling us home. One of the girls turned to me. "Before you go, tell me, do you and Amy still go to that Missionary Settlement? I heard something awful about it."

A few weeks before I had told them of this lovely Settlement where we learned to do embroidery on little, circular wooden frames. "We make flowers so real you think you can pick them," I told them, "and, as for the ladies in charge—" Words failed to express my enthusiasm.

"Well," they all asked now, "what's wrong?"

I hesitated. "The sewing part is as nice as I told you, but the last time we went, Miss Peters, after the sewing, started to talk religion to us, as if we didn't have any ourselves. She told us that Jesus loved us and wanted to save us. Amy and I wanted to stuff our ears. Imagine, she was trying to convert us! Wild horses couldn't drag me there again!"

"That's just what I heard," Miriam answered triumphantly. She seemed rather pleased at my bitter disillusionment.

However well-meaning this Settlement was in its intent, the Jewish children resisted the missionary zeal which motivated some of its leaders. In a few years the missionaries left our neighborhood to exert their influence on less obstinate disciples.

But they did blaze a trail. Soon there were men with vision and money and a great love of America in their hearts, who started a movement to build settlement and neighborhood houses. These neighborhood houses gave the children of the tenements their first experience of club rooms with comfortable chairs, lamps of shining brass and copper. The settlement workers formed reading clubs and debating societies. But, most of all, they gave the children what they needed most, love and understanding.

9

STORY BOOKS AND
REAL STORIES

BOOKS, avidly devoured, were more than food to us.
They stimulated our dreams and enlarged our world.
Drummed into our ears from childhood was the Talmudic
quotation, "An ignorant man cannot be a pious one."

The library was the most wonderful place in the world
for children getting their first taste of books. My friends
and I went to the library mostly for story books, walking ten or fifteen blocks to reach the nearest one. To take
out a book about China or Holland, as children do today,
was unthinkable, even if such books had been available.
We firmly believed that geography (we pronounced it
jography) belonged in the schoolroom, not the library.
We studied about countries in a manner that would cause
amusement to the teacher of today. The class called out
in unison the boundaries of the countries and their
products—wheat, tea, coffee, wool and grain, carefully
memorized, glibly repeated, over and over again. Our

voices could be heard in a loud sing-song, far down the school corridor. The countries were to us just splashes of red, blue or green on the big maps that hung on the wall; of the people who inhabited them, we knew nothing.

My first excursion to the library was to get fairy tales, and in quick succession I devoured them all—Red, Blue, Green, Grimm's, Anderson's. The *Ugly Duckling* was a constant favorite. Standing before the shelves one day, undecided what to choose, helplessly fingering books whose titles fascinated me, I heard someone say, "Wouldn't you like me to help you?" I turned, and there was the librarian smiling at me. She relieved me of the ponderous volume, *The Wandering Jew,* which I had removed from one of the shelves. I gulped my thanks. "There are no more fairy tales on the shelves. My brothers told me to get books by Alger and Henty, but those are boys' books, and I've read some of them. I don't know what to choose."

"Come with me to this section; you will love Louisa Alcott's books."

Soon *Little Women, Little Men, Eight Cousins,* and *An Old-Fashioned Girl* became my gospel, and I looked down upon my friends who were reading *Sink or Swim* and similar books which, until then, I had enjoyed with equal enthusiasm.

Thanks also to this librarian, my reading course was charted. I was soon reading Grace Aguilar, Fenimore Cooper and Dickens, and devoured them with a speed which must have astonished her. She was happily unaware of the generous number of pages that I hurriedly skimmed—pages of description, long, arid stretches that interrupted the more exciting and romantic narrative.

Mama didn't know too much about books. At first I thought she was too busy to care about them, but at times when the house was quiet she would cautiously inquire what we were reading, and would have one of us read out loud. This, I soon discovered, was a pleasure she prized almost as much as listening to us practice the piano or violin.

One evening Mama and I were alone in the dining room. The younger children were in bed, the older boys were out, and Papa had gone to get his beard trimmed—a weekly visit to the barber Mama never permitted him to skip. She was examining and mending table cloths and napkins piled high on the table, and I was deep in my new library book, *The Vale of Cedars*. It was the first time I had read of the persecution of the Jews. I was wiping my eyes and making little snivelling noises, too miserable to get out of my chair to get a handkerchief. "What are you crying about?" Mama asked me. "Isn't there enough trouble in the world without looking for it in books?" "I can't help crying," I said. "This is a story about the Jews in Spain. How could Queen Isabella, who was so good to Christopher Columbus, allow Jews to be burnt at the stake just because they would not become Christians?"

Mama sighed and shrugged her shoulders. "Do not ask me why it was so, or why it still should go on. Ask your Papa how the Jews in Russia tremble under the Czar and his Cossacks, to this very day. When I lived in Poland, just on the border of Germany, pogroms were not unknown either. The great landlords let the peasants starve and then blamed the Jews as the ones responsible for their misery. I remember only one such time. It was just

before Passover. My grandfather, a *rav*, a man of learning and of great human kindness, respected even by the
Polish peasants, heard that an angry mob had gathered
and was shouting for Jewish blood. Grandfather went
to them alone, unafraid. He cried out to them, 'Come, I
will show you how my people live, then you will have
pity in your hearts instead of murder. They are as poor
and as miserable as you.' The crowd listened, and that
pogrom did not take place."

"But why must the Jews always be the ones to suffer,
I don't understand," I said.

"Understand, understand." Mama echoed my words
bitterly. "Do you need to go to Russia or to Poland?
Look what happened in France? You've heard your papa
and everyone talk about the Dreyfus case. Someone sold
French army secrets to Germany. A Captain Dreyfus, a
Jew in the French army, is accused. He's arrested and
after a trial which the whole world called an outrage, he's
sent to Devil's Island. His crime—he was a Jew."

Neither of us spoke for a while. Perhaps we were thinking of the same thing. Persecution was still going on; it
was not a thing of the past. Would it be that way always?

"Mama, would you like me to read to you?"

"Read, read, there's nothing I would like better. Read,"
Mama repeated, as if to herself. "I was not so lucky."

"What do you mean," I asked. "Everyone goes to
school. What is so especially lucky about that?"

"Everyone? No, it is not always possible for everyone.
Take me, for instance. I was not able to go to school.
At least, not for long."

Mama again lapsed into silence. I closed my book. I

wanted to know more. Mama never was one to talk much
—least of all about herself. She put down her sewing,
rested her hand on her cheek, her elbow on the table,
staring straight ahead of her. "But why?" I asked. "Tell
me."

"You wouldn't understand," she said. "I never had a
childhood like other children, for I was the oldest, and
our mother was ailing even before we came to America—
coughing, coughing all the time, and getting thinner, always thinner. 'In America you will be fine,' everyone told
her, as she said goodbye to her mother and father—but
she cried and cried. I guess she knew she would never see
them again."

Mama picked up her sewing. "And then what happened?" I asked.

"I was ten years old when we came to New York.
Israel, my brother, was eight, Annie, the youngest, five
or six, you never knew Annie. She moved far away after
she got married. My father, your *zadie* (grandfather),
got work right away as a mason. We didn't mind anything—the crowded rooms we lived in, Papa coming
home from his work covered with fine dust, which seemed
to make Mama cough more. No, nothing mattered. We
were in America! We started to go to school. The three of
us went. Our mother cooked and washed and ironed, just
like the mothers of other children. I would come home
from school, Mother would be lying down. 'Just resting a
little,' she said. Each week things grew worse.

" '*Mein kindt*,' she said one day, 'I know you should go
out to play, but first go down to the grocery. You will
find the money on the shelf. Buy what is needed—some

bread, eggs, and go to the butcher. Ask for a good piece of flanken—watch that he does not give you all fat and bones. When I am not so tired, I'll make some soup.'

"Each week I stayed home more and more. I was ashamed before the teacher. I could not keep up with girls who were younger than myself. Soon, perhaps it was months, Mother did not get up from bed anymore. Lying there, patient, uncomplaining, she told me how to cook the fish, kosher the meat or the chicken, and prepare it for the Sabbath meal. She seemed almost happy then. 'Come here, little daughter.' She held my hands in hers, now so thin—you could look through them, almost. She smiled sadly at me. . . . 'You are a real *balabuste* (housewife) ; now I need no longer worry for your brother and sister. God is good; for every ill He sends us, He provides a blessing.' It was only a little over a year, and she was gone from us forever."

"And then?" I whispered.

"It is time you were in bed," Mama answered. "I wonder what can be keeping Harry and Ephie!"

The past seemed forgotten in the urgency of the present.

"Will you tell me more some other time?" I insisted.

"Yes, yes. Now help me carry this wash to the closet, and then go to bed."

Later, much later, from bits Mama would tell me, I pieced together the rest of her story. To make up for having to leave school she pored over her brother's lessons night after night. Desperately she tried to learn the mysteries of copy-book and speller, reader and history. It had been a long day for both. She was up at six to shake the stubborn little stove that did both for cooking and heating—the early morning prayers—the breakfast—hurrying brother and sister off to school—preparing the midday meal. Always there was cleaning and cooking, going to market.

"I learned to calculate in my head," she proudly told me, "so that I wasn't cheated, even of a penny. But at night I was too tired to follow the lessons. I put the schoolbooks away . . . for a time."

Five years passed. Mama, now sixteen and wise in the management of the household, sat night after night as she darned and sewed and listened to the talk of her father and the young men he occasionally brought home as his guests.

"My father made no secret of what was in his mind. He thought it high time to look around and find a suitable husband for me. . . . I was now a *calla* (a girl of marriageable age)."

Although Mama protested that "there was plenty of time," she was not averse to looking over the available men suitors. One pleased her most, a tall young man, called Simon, in whom her Papa saw all the desirable traits of a potential son-in-law. Simon not only had a head for business, but he was more learned than the others and could embellish his conversation with the sayings from the Talmud.

"Simon—you mean, Papa!" I interrupted her excitedly. "Did you fall in love at first sight?"

Mama looked at me uncomprehendingly for a moment. Then she smiled. "It didn't happen as it does in your books. I liked him, far better than anyone else—he was not bad looking, had such nice blue eyes. I knew he was good and kind, that he worked hard and wanted to make something of himself. Then he could talk—I guess I liked that best of all. The evenings were long. What was more natural than that he should tell me stories of his life in Russia when he was a boy, of his family, and how it was that he came to America."

"Papa was once a little boy?" I shook my head. I just couldn't believe it. "Papa is forty years old." My friends and I knew that was quite, quite old.

"What was Papa like when he was in Russia?" I persisted. Mama shrugged her shoulders. "I only know what he told me. His was a life like so many others. His mother, poor though she was, wanted him to study, and maybe become a Rabbi when he grew up—but when he was eight years old he was taking care of the horses of a neighboring farmer, for the few kopeks he could earn. He got up at daybreak so that he would have time to go to *cheder*, too."

"Wasn't he afraid the horses might kick him?"

"Afraid? He loved horses," Mama answered. "He cleaned them, gave them their oats and water, sometimes he even rode them. No, he wasn't afraid of horses; they were what you would call friends."

"And did Papa become a rabbi?"

"When he was thirteen years old he was considered a full-grown man. If he wished to study further he had to support himself entirely. So he went to a neighboring city to study with a famous rabbi, and he helped out by teaching the younger children, to pay for his keep. And don't ask what that was, just enough to keep body and

soul together, for the rabbi was poor as a church mouse.
Even this didn't last long. The family needed him at
home, and he went back to Riga. With a pack on his
back, he walked the long, empty stretches of road to sell
the farmers the pots and pans, the ribbons and the cloth
they could not otherwise buy. When things became better,
he went back to his studies, like a see-saw. Perhaps that
might have become his life. He was not unhappy; the
love of study was deep, but he also loved the country,
singing the psalms and the *Shir Ha Shirim* (Song of
Songs) as he walked the lonely roads.

"One day came the news, the news that was always
expected and feared. The Czar was looking for new
conscripts, and Riga would be visited next! To be taken
as a soldier for the Czar could mean twenty years, a
lifetime. Mothers hid their children. 'Where was I to
hide?' he told me. 'Here was I, sixteen years old, and as
strong as an ox!'

Neighbors came in with their own fears, or to give
advice. 'Look,' one of them told him—he held a large
envelope in his hand—'We have another letter from
Berl. Not only does he send us money, but he writes that
soon he will send for us!' Who had not dreamed of
America? The land, a golden land, where one could earn
enough to eat and praise one's own God without
hindrance!

"Then your Papa said, 'All the neighbors looked at
me, and I thought to myself: others have succeeded in
America, why not I?'

"Because his parents feared that he would be taken
forcibly into the army, they were content that he should

go to America. The last ruble was borrowed to provide passage in the steerage. With the help of mujiks and farmers, who hid him and gave him bread to eat, he stole his way, night after night, until he crossed the border into Germany. That's how it was.

"When your Papa sat in our kitchen, he had already been here seven years and had brought over one of his sisters and two brothers. One evening he sat and sat, drinking one glass of tea after another, scarcely opening his mouth. When it was almost time for him to go, he sat twisting his handkerchief between his hands and managed to say, 'At twenty-three a man should be married and have his own home!' And so a few months later we got married."

"But didn't Papa propose?" I asked, a little disappointed at the apparent lack of romance.

"Maybe not in so many words; your Papa was too bashful. But your Papa has shown his love in ways that are better than words. . . . You should never get a worse husband," and she smiled at me thoughtfully.

"And did you open the shop right away?" I asked, trying to picture Mama's story.

"You wouldn't understand. Things don't go so fast. We lived in one room, we cooked and ate in another, and in the third, we cut and sewed the garments, first one kind and then another. After a year, we took a little store. Then, as the business grew, we took a loft for a factory. Abe was born, then Harry. When the baby was eight days old, I was back at the machine. We worked hard and denied ourselves everything. But we went ahead. That's business. You've got to go forward or backward; you can't stand still."

Now I realized why Mama did not know much about books, but what I did not know was her endless striving to gain that which she had missed.

I do not know when or how Mama learned to read. One day I just noticed that Mama was reading. At first it was the easy "Readers" of the younger boys, but later it was novels, the more romantic the better. Perhaps a teacher came to the house while we were busy or out playing. She never told us, and we did not ask.

That certain urge to learn never left her. I recall an incident many years later. As I was about to enter her room I heard voices, hers and that of another. "But, Grandma," I heard a familiar, self-assured, young voice say, "When you say Federation is the only hope to care adequately for our sick, our orphans, or our aged, you must let your voice express what you feel. That is the climax of your speech."

"All right, darling," came the answer. "I'll do it over." I stepped away from the door and left the house. I would not break into their precious secret. I mused as I left—past sixty-five and Mama still anxious to improve her speech, her grammar and her diction.

10

GOING TO THE COUNTRY

AS WE GREW older, the summers seemed to grow
hotter, the streets more and more crowded. Even on East
Broadway, people sat long hours, late into the night,
on the stoops, or took out chairs on the sidewalks, hope-
ful of the breeze that might come from the river. We
didn't seem to mind the heat so much, but Mama and
Papa were troubled and decided that "at least the chil
dren" should leave the hot and dusty city. When Mama
and Papa spoke of our "going to the country," we looked
dubious. It meant separation from the streets we knew
and adventuring into a new world that was strange and
unfamiliar. "Who will we play with? What will we do
there?" To which Mama only replied, "Do? You'll find
plenty to do. Besides, a healthy body means a healthy
mind. You will breathe fresh air."

"What's the matter with the air right here?" Ephie
timidly ventured. Mama's eyes lighted up. "In the
country the air is different." She turned to the older

boys. "When you were babies your Papa and I spent many a night riding on a ferryboat, carrying you in our arms, just that you might get fresh air. For weeks your Papa and I hardly closed an eye. The doctor said that fresh, salt air would keep away summer sickness; so many children had it—so many died, and we were afraid. We could not leave the city, because of the business, so on those hot August nights when our ears were filled with the crying babies tossing on their pillows, we went on the ferry, the one at the foot of Grand Street. Yes, we spent the nights going back and forth, and there were many others, just like us. The air was cool, and the children slept. Fresh air is good."

Mama knew the countryside around Carmel, New Jersey. Papa had a small factory there, and Mama made constant trips to it. Whenever possible, she took Harry with her, bent on teaching him, young as he was, this phase of the business.

It was while on one of these trips that Mama found the farm. She came home excited and jubilant. "I have found just the place you children need. Where is Papa? I want to tell him about it."

"He's upstairs talking to a man, and Aunt Mary is there, too."

Mama shrugged her shoulders. "Still looking for a husband for her, a thankless task. Papa will never learn to leave well enough alone. I thought he learned his lesson after the headache he got sending money to Europe to marry off his sister Reba to that good-for-nothing."

It was no secret to us that Papa for years had been trying to "marry off" Mary, his younger sister, in spite of the misfortune that had followed in the wake of the marriage of Reba, the older sister. Mary had disdained the various matches Papa had proposed. One suitor was too old, another too fat, still another spoke poor English. Now that she worked occasionally in the factory, she was still harder to please, and Mama was annoyed. "Nobody is good enough for her!" Papa's urgency only increased as his brothers were getting married. Again and again Papa had sent for his parents still living in Riga, but their coming was as uncertain as ever. "When the *Rav* gives your sister a *get* (divorce) then please God we will be thankful to come to America." Thus they wrote in a letter Papa had just received. It was clear Mary would have nowhere to live, unless she got a husband. Meanwhile, the matchmaking upstairs was taking a long time.

"What was the farm like, Mama?" I asked, too impatient to wait any longer.

"The farm?" Mama sighed reminiscently. "It wasn't only the farm, but the whole country that I liked. Imagine, every kind of vegetable growing. If you should want a radish, you go out and pick it. You want a tomato? There it hangs on the vine. The corn is almost ripe and ready to be eaten. The apple tree bends under its load of fruit. The farmer has chickens, even ducks— there's a cow and a horse, pigs too. I could *schenk* him (make a present of) the pigs. I could be just as happy without them, they smell enough, but they are not too close to the house. Then there's a well. When you want a drink of water, you just drop the bucket from its cord, turn a wheel, and up it comes—such water I never tasted in my life!

"The farmer's wife took me into the house; it was as clean as gold. She asked me how I had heard about her place. I told her our foreman in the factory thought she might be willing to take my four younger children as boarders. Mrs. Haines, that's her name—the place is called Haines Farm—well, Mrs. Haines and I took to each other like ducks to water. Everything is arranged, and I told her that I would bring the children in a week. The only trouble is, who is going to look after all of you? It's true, you're not babies. David's nearly four years old." Looking at me she said, "When I was eleven years old, my poor mother knew she could depend on me. But it is different today. I would never have a minute's peace of mind—a duck pond and a well! Who knows what mischief Ben and Sidney would be up to!" She sat, her brows knitted in thought.

Papa, Aunt Mary and the strange man then came into the room. Aunt Mary's cheeks were pink, and she looked almost pretty.

"Fannie," Papa said with a smile, "Mr. Kramer and Mary—it's all settled. Mr. Kramer has a nice little store on Second Avenue. He makes a living, and with God's help all will go well. We won't leave it all to God either, we'll help too."

Mama looked pleased. "*Mazeltov,*" she said, kissing Mary, wishing her happiness. Then she brought out the sweet wine and little cakes. We, too, sipped a little of the grape wine reserved usually for the Sabbath and holidays.

After a while Mama returned to the question of the farm. "It is already nearly the end of July, and I told Mrs. Haines that the children would come out next week, but how can they stay there alone?" With a sudden ingratiating smile Mama turned to her sister-in-law. "Look, Mary, you were laid off in the factory. You're not working anyhow. Why don't you go and stay with the children on the farm—it will do you good, too."

Mary turned red and looked helplessly at her Mr. Kramer. She stammered, "We thought—we thought we would get married in a few—" Mama interrupted her. "So you waited so long, you can wait a few weeks longer!" Mr. Kramer nodded his approval, and with many misgivings, Mary agreed to come along and look after us.

The farm, the open spaces, the trees, seeing vegetables grow in neat and tidy rows—it was wonderful! For sheer joy we rolled down little hills that looked as smooth as a carpet, and we were scarcely aware of the stubby grasses which scratched our faces, got into our hair and eyes.

In the barn we climbed up to the hayloft or played "driver and conductor" for hours, taking imaginary journeys on the broken-down wagons and sleighs that cluttered up the place. We were enthralled by the mystery of milk as it gushed out of the cows' udders into the large pail, but we made wry faces when we drank it, still warm. We liked the milk better at home, straight from the grocer!

Poor Aunt Mary ran after us like one of the farmer's own distracted hens. If she expected us to be picking up the eggs out of the straw and coops, we were sure to be near the pigs, watching them in their filthy pen, grunting and squealing.

Mama and Papa took turns, over the Sabbath, to visit us to see if we were getting any fatter, never failing to bring a nicely roasted chicken or a pickled tongue; for we were permitted to eat only the dairy foods and vegetables the farm provided.

There were flies and mosquitoes in abundance. The farm was innocent of screens, but we accepted the buzzing and biting of both, as the price of our happiness at being on a farm.

After four or five weeks we returned home to the familiar streets and to our friends, who examined with a great show of interest the bumps and welts nicely distributed over our faces and legs. The mosquitoes had apparently feasted, but it was some satisfaction, at least, that everyone could see at a glance that we had "been to the country."

The following summer Mama made up her mind to send us to Long Branch to enjoy its cool ocean breezes. A boarding house was found, glorified by the name of "Ocean View Hotel," highly recommended by one of Mama's friends who clasped her hands in ecstacy as she regaled us with a description of the food served there. "Such a table!" she exclaimed. Her eyes rolled heavenwards. "The food just melts in your mouth. And what is more," she said, "you won't have to worry. Mrs. Levins is a motherly soul, who will look after your children as if they were her own." To Mama such a combination was irresistible.

As soon as school was over, a huge trunk was brought

from the shop. It was a trunk used ordinarily to carry the boxes of samples for the salesmen, and was plastered all over with stickers and labels of journeyings from New York to Los Angeles. Every few days, dresses, petticoats, boys' suits, underwear, stockings and handkerchiefs would be dropped into its cavernous depths. Closed at last by the simple process of three of us sitting on the lid, it was carted away to the pier. The great day of departure arrived; for us, all the more exciting because, going by steamboat, we would sail right out on the Atlantic Ocean. Up at the crack of dawn, dressed hours ahead of time, starched and uncomfortable, at length we made our way to the pier, all of us carrying satchels, valises and boxes, one of which contained the lunch to be eaten on the boat. We came early, because Mama wisely anticipated a crush, but so apparently did everyone else. There was a wild scramble for the pile of folded carpet-covered chairs, and after we secured them, we deposited our bundles at the choicest spot still available. Leaving Mama and Papa to guard our possessions, we raced all over the boat. Up the steep gangway to the upper deck —we stared inquisitively at the captain, as he stood in his little, glass-enclosed pilot house, only to be suddenly chased away by a seaman who angrily pointed to a sign, "Passengers Forbidden To Enter."

Undismayed, we made for the bottom of the ship where we could see the engines quietly throbbing. A glance at the shining steel and brass was enough for me, but Ben was not to be moved; he just looked and looked, his whole being absorbed in the mystery of what made the wheel turn. It was only my final threat to leave him there alone that succeeded in getting him to accompany the rest of us to our places on the deck.

A fine haze hung over the Bay; at nine o'clock it was already unbearably hot. People were fanning themselves with large palm fans, wiping their sweaty faces, waiting for the breeze that was so slow in coming. As the boat nosed past the Statue of Liberty, everyone leaned over to get a better view of it, especially the older folks, who kept staring long after it had disappeared from our sight.

The sky thickened and grew black. There was a flash of lightning and the rumble of thunder. Mama and Papa, sitting on the uncomfortable little chairs, began wearily to hand out sandwiches and hard-boiled eggs, after our repeated and insistent reminders that we were hungry. We had now reached the open sea. We looked with wonder —just sea and sky and our boat cutting a white path through the water. With half-eaten sandwiches we edged our way among the crowd to the rail, where we could watch the churning foam. The wind suddenly freshened, and in a few minutes it seemed we were in the teeth of a gale. Mama came over to us, asking angrily if we wished to be blown into the water, and herded us back to our chairs just as the rain began to fall in torrents. Sheets of water coming in every direction flooded our valises and bundles. Again there was a mad scramble as everyone hurriedly picked up his scattered belongings and rushed for the other side of the boat, already packed and crowded.

The *Mary Patten* creaked and groaned, the engines pounded and then suddenly stopped altogether. A sailor edged his way into the crowd, shouting, "Boat's listing, get to the other side of the boat." Nobody moved, the salon inside was crowded to suffocation, and no one wished to risk going back to the rain and wind off the storm side of the boat. "Look," cried one of the men, "they're throwing our baggage overboard!" Those who could leaned far over the rail to see what was happening. Sure enough there was a splash and then another and another—they were throwing the trunks overboard! I couldn't see, but it seemed that the last one must be ours. All those dresses that Mama had sewn for me night after night, and my new coat that I had not put on even once!

The boat was dipping so crazily now you could hardly stand up. Again sailors pushed in among the crowd and without a word, herded us to the other side. When one woman protested that she and her baby would get soaking wet from the rain, he answered grimly, "You'll get much wetter if the boat goes down." Word flew around like wildfire. "Get on the life preservers." But where were they? No one knew. Mama turned angrily to Papa. "Don't stand there—go find them. See where they are." Papa soon came back with life preservers, staggering under their weight. Everyone had them now, and was desperately trying to put them on. Children were crying everywhere. Mama and Papa were clutching us with cold and trembling hands. As we looked at their faces we felt terror creep upon us. We realized now for the first time that this was perhaps more than the "adventure" we had been so hopefully anticipating.

The whistle of the boat sang out its shrieking note again and again. The blast each time made me shake with fright. The air seemed to vibrate with the sound of that last despairing cry. In the tense silence that followed I could hear people saying, "She'll go down in an hour, it's the engine—" "We'll pull through all right, if this gale lets up—" "She's nothing but an old tub." "The steamship company, a curse upon them, they ought to rot in hell—" "It's an outrage—" and mutterings and prayers, "Oh, God, take pity on my poor children—"

Suddenly there was a shout, a howl as if hundreds of people had been released from unbearable pain. "A boat!" they yelled, "a boat is coming; we are saved!"

There, steaming toward us was a tug. It looked like a toy from where I stood. Breathlessly we watched. It was coming closer and closer—then it was beside us. Sailors suddenly appeared from nowhere, and ropes were thrown. There was cursing and swearing as the ropes fell in the water, then were caught and made fast. The rain had stopped, the wind died down, the tug was moving, and we with it! There was another shout of joy. "We're moving, we're going! Thank God—God be praised!" An hour and a half later we limped into the pier at Long Branch, three hours behind schedule. The fear and terror had passed.

All the passengers were no sooner on shore than there was a general clamor about the baggage.

"Simon, wait for me here with the children. I'm going to find out what happened to our trunk."

"It's no use, Mama," I said "they threw ours overboard, it was so big." Papa shrugged his shoulders. "What does it matter, as long as we are all safe and sound?"

"Matter?" Mama said, "Do you think the children can run around naked?"

Without another word, she disappeared into the hold of the ship. Shortly after, there came Mama, followed by two huskies, carrying the trunk between them. As they dumped it on the dock next to us, they cheerfully remarked, "Youse were just lucky, that's all."

The next day was warm and beautiful, and we could hardly wait to get down to the beach. We took turns undressing in the tiny bathhouse engaged for the purpose, and Mama marshalled us down to the water's edge. The boys had on one-piece, striped wool suits, the pants dangling far below their knees. My bathing suit which modestly covered me from the neck to below my knees, was of navy blue wool, and the large sailor collar, as well as the gathered skirt, was generously trimmed with white braid. The skirt, already long (Mama always looked ahead), stretched to my ankles once it touched the water.

Mama looked grand. Her bathing suit of black heavy poplin had been made by a dressmaker and fitted her well. Her natural curves were decourously held in by the heavily boned corset which she and all women of a certain avoirdupois wore without complaint under their suits. Decency was further emphazised: her suit covered her bosom and arms, long black stockings encased her feet, and a rougish-looking mother-hubbard hat with a ruffle made her hair secure from spray or sand. Papa remained at the hotel. He loathed sea water bathing and could never understand people's mania for dressing and undressing several times a day.

As we inched our way into the water, Mama told us we must all learn to swim, herself included. "I have already spoken to the bathing-master. After next week, perhaps, when you are more accustomed to the water, he will take you in one at a time and teach you the breast stroke— but until we know how, we must hold onto the ropes."

On Sunday evening, as Mama and Papa were preparing to leave to return to the city, this time by train, I was given a series of instructions. "Remember, ten minutes in the water is enough; then they are to dress quickly. It's different for me," Mama said. "If I stay in the water for a half hour or longer, I can afford to lose a few pounds. The main thing is that you hold onto the ropes."

Jumping into the foaming waves, picking purple and silvery shells on the yellow sand, watching the setting sun, like a huge ball of fire, dip beyond the horizon into the sea, was lovely beyond words. But such joys were dimmed and forgotten as I stood on the beach, wildly waving and calling by name my three mischievous younger brothers. They had discarded the ropes at once as fit only for sissies, and the ten minutes so meticulously commanded by Mama had lengthened into an hour. Anxiously I stood there, calling with all my might, "Ben! Sidney! David!" As they ducked into the waves they would be lost to view and then would reappear. Cold and shivering, my wet bathing suit clinging to me, I shouted and shouted, but my voice was lost in the roar of wind and water. My oft repeated threat to tell Mama was useless. They understood perfectly that if I told on them, Mama would forbid us to bathe altogether and would certainly take the bathing suits with her to the city. Only on the weekends, when the rest of the family arrived, could I shed my responsibility and thoroughly enjoy myself.

After four weeks we returned to the city, our faces and arms a deep chocolate brown. We had a reunion with Aunt Belle, Uncle Israel and our cousins. Aunt Belle eyed me disapprovingly. "She's as thin as a broomstick. Fannie, there is only one place to build up children," she said with finality, "the mountains," and she looked fondly at her girls, who looked prettier and plumper than ever after their summer vacation in the Catskills.

11

VISITING

COMING HOME from school one day, I found Grandpa waiting for me. "It's a good thing you came now; I was just leaving."

"What's your hurry, *Zadie?*" I said. "It's still early. Did you have something to eat or drink?" I inquired, suddenly mindful of Mama's hospitable example. "Yes, yes," he smiled at me. "I had everything—a glass of tea with lemon and a piece of your mother's yeast cake left over from *Shabbus* (Sabbath). Nobody can beat your Mama's *challa* or her yeast cake. But I must go soon. I promised to bring home a few things that 'she' needs for supper."

That 'she' needs! I knew who that meant. Once I asked Mama, "who cooks for Grandpa when he doesn't come here?" "He has a wife," Mama answered shortly.

"Why doesn't she come to visit us, too?"

I got no reply, and Mama's face didn't encourage further questions. I wanted to ask if Grandpa's wife was now her mother and my grandma, but somehow I could not. I

89

remembered how sad Mama became whenever she spoke of her "little mother whom God had not intended long for this world."

Yet I wanted to see Grandpa's wife. "*Zadie*," I began, "would you like me to walk home with you and make a little visit?"

"What a question, *narrele* (little fool)!" he answered. "But *mach es geschwind* (make it snappy)—maybe we will meet the hoky-poky ice cream man on the way; I know what a sweet tooth you have."

I took Grandpa's arm. It was fun to go out together. It meant stopping whenever I wished and being treated to all the good things displayed by vendors on their carts: a sliver of luscious watermelon, ice-cream dabbed on a bit of paper, an ear of corn taken out of a steaming kettle and liberally sprinkled with salt and butter, chestnuts roasting in their blackened tin ovens over the charcoal burner, and best of all the taffy-apple with its hard sugar coating of dazzling red. Every season had its appointed goodies as I had discovered when out walking with my *Zadie*.

Many of my friends had a grandmother or a grandfather living with them. Often it meant uncomfortable crowding, but to send an aged parent to a charity "home" was unthinkable, a disgrace to the family. My cousin Rose had a grandfather so old he was almost bent double. Rose whispered to me, "He sits in his chair all day, studying the Talmud; he even forgets when it is time to eat." His long white beard covered his chest and rested like a fringe on the book he was studying.

But my grandfather wasn't nearly so old, and maybe

not so learned or pious. He was tall and vigorous looking, his short beard was red and curly, and there was a merry twinkle in his eyes. He was proud that he needed to depend on no one, that he was still able to ply his trade of mason and builder.

Walking now next to him, I found it difficult to keep up with his stride, and I was glad when we reached Allen Street where he lived. The elevated thundered overhead, the pillars and tracks shut out the sky, and the street looked gloomy even on a sunny day. I peered into the dark basements as we hurried by, and I found their dinginess aglow with the display of brass and copper candlesticks and samovars and huge pots swinging by their long, burnished handles. I did not know then that Allen Street had already become the market for old world brass and copper.

We stopped at a nondescript flat and walked up two flights of stairs in a dark hallway. Grandpa gave an imperious knock on the door of his flat, and it flew open. I could hardly make out the figure of the woman who stood before us. The light shining in my eyes, after groping in the dark hallway, made me blink.

"See whom I have brought here," Grandpa said to the figure bobbing before us. "A special guest." As I looked at her, she quickly put her arms around me and made funny little exclamations to show her pleasure. "What a dear guest!" and she wagged her head comically from side to side. She led me into the room. I had to sit in the big overstuffed chair near the window, and she kept looking at me as if I were something precious. The windows were on a level with the elevated tracks, and the sky was no longer hidden. The room was bright and cheerful and immaculately clean, judged even by my Mama's standards.

"You must be tired; it is a long walk from your house to us." She spoke a mixture of English and Yiddish which I easily understood. I scarcely listened; I was examining her quite unabashed, taking in the kindly, plump face, the long, dark dress, and the black apron embroidered in many colors, unlike any I had ever seen. I looked inquisitively at her *sheitel*, the ritual wig she wore out of piety. It was wavy and crimped, not too unbecoming. Altogether I thought, after my scrutiny, she's nice, very nice, not very old, either.

"Are you my *Bubbe* (grandmother)?" I began. I stopped, shy at having said something that vaguely I felt I might have better left unasked. "Not exactly," she murmured. "I am *stief-grossmutter*. Your mother's mother is dead many years—I knew her. The year she came from Poland we were neighbors."

Strange thoughts rushed through my mind. Then you knew my real Grandma! Were you kind and good to the brave, sick grandmother my Mama told me about? Did she like you? These questions and others were at the tip of my tongue. Grandpa seemed to read my thoughts. He broke in suddenly, "You know, I'm thirsty; how about a nice glass of tea and some *eingamachs* (orange preserves) for all of us?"

"Woe is me, I had quite forgotten!" step-grandma exclaimed. "You will, my child, drink a *glassele* tea with us?" and she started to bustle about the room. "What *mazel* (luck). Only yesterday I baked a honey cake and a sponge cake!"

"Are you going to make tea in the samovar?" I had noticed a very large one sitting in lonely splendor on a side table. We had one at home, too, but I had never seen it in use.

"No, my child," she answered, "you would be weary waiting for the charcoal to burn; the kettle is on the stove; that will be much faster."

She then moved the rubber plant from the table, and set it on the window ledge. She covered the table with a fancy embroidered cloth and set out with the cakes a dish of preserves made of orange peel, honey and nuts, and placed another bowl of apples in the center. I sipped the hot tea from a tall glass without the usual risk of burning my fingers, because of the cunningly wrought filigree metal container in which the glass was resting.

"I never saw anything as nice as these," I said.

"They came from Russia," she said, and she seemed pleased that I noticed such things. The elevated rumbled past, and the vibration seemed to shake the house. When it was quiet again, she continued, "In Russia everyone loves tea and drinks it often, perhaps because it is so cold there for many long months. On *simchas* (festive occasions), one adorns the tea table with a specially fine box of silver for the tea leaves, a glass or silver plate for the preserves, and silver-plated glass holders, finer even than these, for the glasses of tea that one may sip it scalding hot. But you are not eating anything!" In truth, I was struggling with the cake, which I found hard and dry. "Take some more *eingemachs*," she urged, "it will do you good. When I was as young as you, I used to put a whole spoonful right in my tea."

I was glad Grandpa's wife was doing all the talking, for I still did not know how to address her. Besides, I kept thinking of the Grandma who had died so young. Yet it was nice, I thought, that Grandpa had his snug little home, instead of being crowded with us. I felt very old and wise as I said to myself, "I understand how Mama feels. She cannot bear to have anyone take her own Mother's place."

That's it! That was why she wouldn't have my step-grandma come to our house! When I come home this afternoon, I will tell Mama how good and kind my step-grandma is.

Engrossed in my own thoughts, I scarcely heard her questions. "How is your Mama? And your Papa?" I nodded absentmindedly, as she murmured, "God be thanked for their good health."

"Sophele," began Grandpa, "you seem to have lost your tongue, but you," and he turned smiling to 'her', "you make up for both."

"It is not often one of your grandchildren comes here to visit," and she raised her shoulders and sighed deeply.

"Would you like to hear about school?" I asked, determined to cheer her up. She nodded encouragingly. "Your Zadie tells me you play the piano, that you read from the Bible, and that you are smart in school, too."

"No, I'm not smart, just middling, but being smart isn't everything, is it? I could never be mean as some girls are. A few days ago a new girl came into our class. I noticed her standing alone; no one spoke to her during recess. I went over and asked her if she wanted to play tag with us. When I told the other girls, they said they didn't want a greenhorn to spoil their game. So I didn't play either. The next day when she raised her hand for permission to go to the yard, not one of the girls sitting near her offered to go with her. You see, there's a rule that no one can go alone to the yard until the workmen get through fixing the toilets. The new girl was nearly crying, she had to go so bad. I raised my hand, jumped up from my seat way down front, and went with her."

Grandpa's wife shook her head sympathetically. "You don't know what a good deed you did. A stranger in the school, frightened, lonely—suddenly she finds a friend." She thoughtfully bit into the lump of sugar and took another mouthful of tea. "You are going to be her friend?" She raised her eyebrows, inquiringly.

"Yes, of course I am—Amy, that's what the teacher called her, and she's just as pretty and sweet as her name."

Grandpa's wife took my hand. She looked at me and said, "You will be the friend of many. Many will turn to you, my dear child."

It was now time to leave. Grandpa put on his coat and was waiting to take me home. As we stood in the doorway saying goodbye, step-grandma went back into her room. She took a large red apple from the table, polished it with her apron, and gave it to me. "Take it, my child, and don't forget to come again."

"I will, I will," I easily promised.

I looked up as we reached the ground floor. There she was, still standing, looking down the deep well of the staircase, smiling and urging me to come again soon.

I meant to go there again, but there was homework,

piano lessons, and dancing school. There were friends to see and games to be played, and the long walk to the library.

Did Mama, I wonder, say something to Grandpa after I told her about my visit? I never knew. And so step-grandma receded completely into the dream world, from which I now recall her.

I can still see her polishing the apple and giving it to me as if it were a precious jewel. "Take it, *mein kindt.*"

I never saw her again.

12

CONVALESCING

IN THOSE DAYS, it seems in retrospect, winters
came earlier, and they lasted longer. Older people spoke
of them as hard and bitter. This winter was no exception,
even we children had our fill of snow and ice. The huge
snowman my brothers had made in our areaway had
shrunk to a wizened little figure; only the two coals for
his eyes and the battered hat on his head reminded us of
his former glory. We had enough of sliding on the icy
film that was our substitute for skating or of watching
horses helplessly struggling to keep their footing, then
fall, to lie, panting, until a driver came who was skilled
enough to help them rise again. Suddenly the fury of
the March winds was spent, the sun shone with warming
promise, and we children complained loudly of our
woolen underwear, giving unmistakable proof of our
discomfort by scratching our arms and legs.

There was no doubt of it—spring was here at last.
The bush in our backyard bravely put forth its first

tender leaves and the younger members of the family blossomed forth in an assortment of ills. When they got well it was my turn to be ill.

Dr. Horn, on his first visit to our house, ordered castor oil—as usual. This infallible remedy, a good, stiff dose given in a cup of steaming hot coffee, was prescribed for everyone unlucky enough to have to be in bed; it had to be swallowed, no matter how the body or the spirit rebelled.

After two weeks, the Doctor was making his last visit. He closed his leather bag with a snap and told Mama to "feed her up," and then, as an afterthought, "Not so much reading—"

Already late for business, Mama prepared to leave, putting everything I could need within easy reach of the bed. I readily promised that I wouldn't read, as I had finished my last library book, *Uncle Tom's Cabin,* that very morning while my little brothers were fast asleep. Alone now, I relived the story, and the tears that had sprinkled the pages of the book easily fell again.

I took up my slate and my slate pencil and began to play tick-tack-toe, but it was no fun to beat one's self. I could hear Emma below washing dishes, and the clatter of the pots and pans. Once in a while I could hear her voice as it came up to me on the wave of a song, sad and foreign.

"If only Emma weren't so busy," I thought to myself. I picked up a stocking from Mama's basket, one with a gaping hole, stretched it over a water glass, as Mama had shown me, and started to mend it. "I'll surprise Mama and finish it," I thought, feeling a glow of self-righteousness. I wove the black threads in and out, over and under. It was no use. "Darning stockings is much harder on the eyes than reading," I reasoned with myself, "and not nearly so pleasant." I put the stocking away.

Suddenly, out of the stillness, I heard music that rattled and almost shook the window pane. It was the German band. I recognized it immediately, for it often came into the neighboring back yards. There could be no mistaking the yodeling singer and the umpah umpah of the big horn. They were now playing the waltzes and folk songs of their motherland.

As the musicians were blowing and puffing away in the yard, I saw windows going up all around. Women leaned out and threw down pennies wrapped in paper. The music makers caught the pennies and bowed low, as if on a stage. The neighbors were as pleased as I was with the music; suddenly, everyone, it seemed, had to hang out the wash. The clotheslines were attached to a great pole, planted in the yards for just that purpose, and the pulleys squeaked as the women drew the lines to them. Soon the sky was nearly blotted out by a mass of billowing sheets and long underwear, as the neighbors, leaning out of their windows, talked and smiled to one another and urged the band to play "just once more."

When the musicians had exhausted their repertoire and had collected as much money as they could, they left as suddenly as they had come. I could hear them faintly begin again, as they invaded some other back yard further down the street.

The morning didn't seem too long after that; hucksters came into the yard, calling their wares. One spry old

fellow climbed half way up the clothes pole, shouting something that sounded like "ca . . ole . . cloo." It wasn't until years later that I learned he had been offering "cash for old clothes" in his weird and plaintive call.

Mama and my oldest brother came from the shop for midday dinner, and the others from school. Soon they were all gone again. The afternoon settled down to a dreary wait until three o'clock. Surely, I thought, some of the girls would come to see me. Before I could meditate too long on the fickleness of friends, I heard the slamming of the gate in our basement, and a minute later my cousin Rose came in, her books dangling from a long leather strap.

As always, she was nibbling candy from a paper bag. I was so happy to see her. She offered me the bag, her mouth too full for the usual salutations. I selected a long licorice "shoestring," and we were both silent for a while, savoring the bittersweet taste. I liked Rose—there was something about her that was different, a wistful sadness in her that touched some unknown spring in me. She played the piano better than anyone I knew, even better than my brother Abe, and when she spoke of her music, her eyes brightened.

After we talked a while I asked, "What happened after I left your house—you remember, just before I got sick? Is your papa going to let your brother Oscar go to Art School?" She shook her head. "After you went home, Papa lost his temper and tore all of Oscar's drawing and charcoal sketches, even the one he made of Grandpa for his eightieth birthday. Mama tried to prevent him, but he wouldn't listen. He told Oscar he wasn't going to have a lazy, good-for-nothing sit around the house, and that he should go out and work. It's awfully sad for Oscar. He just hates working in the store—and papa has so much on his mind, too. Something's gone wrong with his business —he worries night and day."

Just as we were in the most interesting part of the conversation, another cousin, May, came in, and Rose shut up like a clam. She knew that May's family agreed with her papa about Oscar.

May was the fashion-plate among the girls of the family, and looked as if she were dressed for a party even when she was going to school. She wanted to know all about my brother Harry's coming *Bar Mitzvah*. Only too willingly I launched into a description of the preparations. The caterer had come several times, and Mama had gone over the menu with her time and again. All the boys had brand new suits, hats and shoes bought especially for the occasion. The dressmaker, Mrs. Toff, who lived next door, was making Mama a "creation," and my dress was to be a twin of my cousin Sylvia's, only in light blue instead of pink. Mama would have had it finished if I had not taken sick with tonsilitis.

As for the presents, they were just too wonderful! Harry had received six inkwells already, one more magnificent than the other, with pearl or silver pens to match. I can't remember how many stickpins came, resting in little plush boxes, and link buttons for his cuffs. And books—two enormous volumes of Shakespeare, with pictures called engravings, and a whole set of Henty and a lovely, leather-bound book of poems by somebody called Wordsworth! All the first and second cousins were going to be invited to the evening party, but Mama couldn't bother sending invitations to children—they would just come. I stopped for breath. Why didn't girls become *Bar Mitzvah!* We solemnly agreed that it wasn't only the presents, but such a haul was not to be lightly brushed aside.

All too soon, May and Rose had to leave, and I was alone once more. I looked at the yard in the fading light. It was quiet, just cats creeping along our fence on their own mysterious business. Fascinated, I watched their stealthy, graceful movements. A big tomcat, a stranger, came prowling into their private domain, and the air was filled with terrifying howls, screeching and caterwauling. Again the windows of the neighbors all around flew open, and hot water was poured from buckets, and missiles thrown to chase away the maurauders.

In no time at all Mama and the others came home, and the house was full of pleasant excitement.

What became of Oscar? He never became a painter. He did nothing—was a failure. But a curious thing happened. His little brother, who was only two years old at the time, as he reached fifteen or sixteen, began to draw and paint as Oscar had done before him. Perhaps because of the futile struggle that Oscar had made, Paul, the younger brother, was determined to succeed. Nothing stopped him. Without money, without friends, encouraged only by the limitless faith and love of his mother, he plodded on, and today he is a well-known American painter.

13

HARRY BECOMES A MAN

HARRY'S BAR MITZVAH was grander than I had expected. The Synagogue that Saturday morning was crowded with family, relatives and friends, all dressed in their best. I sat upstairs with Mama in the gallery reserved for women. The view below was completely shut off by the yellow silk curtains which stretched in front of us across the gallery rail. I pushed the curtain in front of me to one side. Once before I had attempted to do this, but had been indignantly reminded by an old crone, in a voluble mixture of Yiddish and English, that it was "sinful to distract men from the worship of God by the sight of women." Mama had said nothing at the time, but later she told Papa she had no patience with such fanatics. "The curtains in the *Schule* will disappear just as surely as *sheitels* (wigs) have disappeared." On this Sabbath, however, of my brother's *Bar Mitzvah,* there was no one to admonish me, and Mama and all those who sat near me craned their necks, delighted to take advantage of my heretical behavior.

Wrapped in their prayer shawls, a long procession of men approached the Ark where the scrolls of the Law of Moses were kept. A chorus of boys' voices, seeming to come from nowhere, filled the synagogue and joined with the voice of the cantor as he sang, "Out of Zion shall go forth the Law and the Word of the Lord from Jerusalem."

Then the cantor, in impressive tones, summoned the *Bar Mitzvah*. There was a hush of expectancy as he ascended the altar.

That's what Papa had meant when I had asked him a few nights before, "What is a *Bar Mitzvah?*" "It's about time you knew," he had answered impatiently. "When a boy is thirteen years old and is able to take his part in the service in *Schule*, he is then a *Bar Mitzvah*, no longer a child, but a man responsible for all his future deeds."

I looked at Harry as he stood at the reading desk, the great scroll of the Law of Moses open before him. I sighed, 'And now he is a man responsible—' He began chanting the text in a high, nasal key, and bearded men shook their heads with approval of this new son of Israel. But all this was only preliminary to his reading of the *Haftorah*, a chapter from the Prophets. His voice became more assured, no longer the high sing-song chant considered traditional in reading from the Law. In a sweet voice he intoned his portion from the prophet Zachariah "not by might, nor by power, but by my spirit, saith the Lord." Mama beamed with pride. I am sure she saw in her son another battler for the Lord. I glanced down to where

Papa was sitting, and I could see the faraway look on his face, as if he were dreaming of the days when he had walked the roads in Russia chanting the Psalms out loud, not only to give himself courage, but also for the sheer beauty of the poetry.

When the service neared the end, the rabbi blessed the *Bar Mitzvah* with the traditional blessing, and the whole congregation gathered around to congratulate him, as well as Mama and Papa.

Nearly everyone trooped to our house for the *Kiddush* and refreshments. They consumed vast quantities of *gefülte* fish and all manner of little cakes. The next evening there was a further celebration, an elaborate dinner for the relatives and friends, the party to which I had been looking forward for so many weeks. Long tables had been set up that Sunday morning in our parlor after all the gold furniture had been carefully stacked in the basement or brought upstairs to the neighbors. I wore my pale blue dress, and cousin Sylvia wore her pale pink. All the cousins, first and second, were there and sat at a special children's table, because the caterer told Mama it wouldn't cost as much.

After we had eaten till we could hardly move, the cantor chanted the Grace, a very long one. As if that were not enough, he added a few Psalms for good measure.

Then came the entertainment. Mrs. Rose, one of Mama's dearest friends, sang in a deep, throaty voice a piece everyone seemed to recognize, about Samson and Delilah. I knew it was lovely by the way everybody clapped. I wasn't listening too intently—I was so busy watching the way she opened her mouth, as wide as possible, calling desperately for Samson.

Another friend of the family, a lawyer, was now called upon. Before he started his speech, he told some jokes that made everyone laugh. Then he began his oration. He was wonderful, too. He looked just like the big boys in the school assembly when they stood on the platform and recited, "Give me liberty or give me death!" As he sat down he wiped his forehead with Mama's large dinner napkin while everyone applauded furiously. "He's a regular Daniel Webster!" they kept repeating.

The principal of Harry's school was there too, but he just rose from his chair and patted Harry's shoulders. The violin teacher, Mr. Lewando, after some coaxing, consented to play a duet with Harry, whom he called "my gifted pupil." He and Harry had been practicing the piece for weeks and weeks, so why, I wondered, did he need to be coaxed? There were more speeches, and everyone kept repeating the same thing, that Harry ought to go to college and be a lawyer, "he has such a head on him." Mama looked at Papa. She seemed troubled. They already had decided that Harry would go to the shop as soon as he graduated, as had his brother, Abe. Why were their friends putting ideas in Harry's head?

At last Harry arose to make his speech. He thanked his teachers for all they had done for him, and then he turned to Mama and Papa. In a choked voice he recalled their loving care through countless "sleepless nights." "I will try to repay you," he said, "follow in your footsteps. To help one's fellow man, to be a good citizen, to be God-fearing and just, those are the ideals dear to Mama and Papa. In time I hope they will become mine."

There were tears on Mama's face, and Papa loudly blew his nose. I knew what Mama and Papa were thinking. Had I not heard them talking of it again and again? The business needed Harry's young strength and that of his brothers; it would grow because of them. In that hard school the boys would make a place for themselves in the world and learn their responsibilities to their fellow-men, and reach out for the things of the spirit, as well.

Were we a religious family? I hardly know. There was no compulsion, no strict insistance on religious observance in our home. The boys went to synagogue and studied in *cheder* (Hebrew school), but girls were not expected to be either very learned or pious. It was considered enough if they went to services for a few hours on the festivals and the high holy days. On Yom Kippur, Papa, with the older boys, would leave the house at seven-thirty in the morning for synagogue, and would remain there all day. Mama would follow a few hours later with a parting injunction to me to be sure to "break my fast" with Ben anl Sidney not later than twelve o'clock. I said that I wanted to fast the whole day like my older brothers, to which Mama curtly replied, "You have time enough to be a *tzaddick* (saint)."

After our parents had left for synagogue a whole flock of girls gathered in our back yard or walked the deserted streets, arm in arm. Time fairly crawled; we gazed at the big clock set in the pointed spire of the Hoe factory near the river—only ten o'clock! It had been ages since we had last eaten, five-thirty of the evening before, and then only plain boiled, unsalted chicken and soup, so as to forestall suffering from thirst. Even a sip of water was forbidden, once the fast was begun. No matter what we started to talk about, it invariably ended in a description of our favorite foods, punctuated by inquiries as to "how do you feel," as we had heard our elders inquire of each other during the day of fasting. By twelve-thirty our boasts of waiting yet another hour would noticeably diminish, and gradually each of us would disappear into her home and shamefacedly surrender the glory of longer martyrdom.

Later in the afternoon I went to the synagogue to visit Mama. I squeezed into the crowded bench next to her. It was hot and stuffy, and except for a little pat and a furtive kiss, my presence was scarcely noted. The drone of praying voices and the tear-stained faces communicated to me the awful solemnity of the day. From the women's gallery where I sat I could peep down through the curtains and see the men covered in their large praying shawls, a vast throng of swaying bodies. Their voices broke out again and again in a loud, agonized prayer, then subsided into a dull murmur. Above it all, I heard the clear, piercing voice of the cantor who trilled and trilled, as if to charm the ear of the Almighty Himself. After an hour or more of being alternately squeezed and admonished to "shush," as I felt the irrepressible urge to talk, I was glad to leave and go back to my friends.

I always returned to the services before sundown, so that I could hear the last blast of the *shofar* (ram's horn) and join in the words: "The Lord thy God, the Lord is

One." Repeated seven times by the whole congregation, at the top of their voices, this resembled a roar which strangely thrilled me. It was a confession of faith, a shout of joy, a mystic belief in the goodness and oneness of God.

The great fast, feared and anticipated, was over. Everyone now made a wild scramble to fold prayer shawls, collect prayer books, and hurry home.

No matter how we hurried, Mama was there before us to see that everything was in readiness. The table literally groaned with food. Papa came, washed his hands, put on his hat, and in leisurely fashion began the blessing over the wine. The boys hungrily eyed the platters of fish, the loaves of homemade *challa*, the bowl of fruit.

"Simon," said Mama, in what was supposed to be a whisper, "hurry up. Enough is enough! The children are hungry."

Papa finished off in a quick jumble of indistinguishable sounds.

"Amen," we chorused eagerly, and we fell ravenously upon our food.

The older boys seemed annoyed that we, the unregenerate, half-day fasters, demanded and consumed as much food as they did. "Gosh," said Abe querulously, "you'd think they fasted like us. Say, kid," he said, turning to me, "what makes you so hungry? Didn't you enjoy your lunch?"

"I'm fasting a whole day next year; I don't care what Mama says."

"Oh," said Abe pleasantly, "just laying in a supply a year ahead of time."

"Mama," I began, ready to cry.

"Leave the child alone," Papa said. "Maybe she's growing."

"Maybe she's growing a tapeworm," Abe muttered under his breath.

Bar Mitzvahs, festivals, fast days—was this all we knew of religion? Was there nothing more? What of the prayers we read over and over and understood so little? To love justice; to do righteously, to walk humbly before God; to remember the poor, the orphan and the widow. Did some of these commands from the Bible seep down into the deep consciousness we call our souls? I believe they did. But the ceremonies and observances of the Synagogue and the home gave color and substance to what I fear would otherwise have been, for us children at least, cold and meaningless moral laws.

14

DANCING SCHOOL

EVERY SATURDAY throughout the fall and
winter my cousins Rose and May would call for me to go
to Brooks' Dancing School. As soon as our basement bell
would ring, I hastily left the table, put on my hat and
coat, picked up my dancing slippers and shouted a hurried goodbye to the family, still engrossed in the Sabbath
meal.

"You haven't even touched your apple strudel," Mama
would remonstrate.

"It won't be wasted, Mama, Sidney will eat it," and
Sidney, the *nascher* (lover of sweets) invariably did.

We started out, excited and happy, our arms linked,
a little conscious of being dressed in our best. Our dancing
slippers dangled in bags from our wrists.

We cut through dingy Clinton and Hester Streets,
empty of pushcarts, strangely peaceful because of the
Sabbath. We reached Grand Street, crowded and lively,
lined with fine shops. Suddenly we stopped to stare into

the windows of Lord and Taylor, Kurzmans and Ridleys. May, whose mother had been brought up in Savannah, spoke with authority whenever it was a question of clothes or style. Rose and I listened respectfully.

"You see that black lace gown there, and the pink moire taffeta? Those are what the Southern belles wear when they go to balls," said May. Her eyes rested on a black velvet cape trimmed with tiny ermine tails. "That's what I want when I get married."

Half way to Brooks' we stopped at an ice cream parlor gleaming with dark wood and imitation marble. Ice cream soda was something brand new, and we were wild about it. We settled ourselves on the tall, revolving stools at the counter.

"Well, young ladies," said the fat little man behind the counter, "what will it be today?" Rose and I looked at each other, then back at him, fascinated by his hair, set symmetrically in waves and plastered on his forehead. We exchanged triumphant glances. It *was* a wig—our doubts were laid at rest.

"Well! Well! Young ladies?" he repeated, smiling.

"I'll have vanilla."

"Make mine a strawberry, with strawberry ice cream." It was only I who suffered agonies of indecision. "I'll— I'll have a chocolate with chocolate cream." Slowly we sipped our drinks and ecstatically rolled the huge lumps of ice cream on our tongues. No one spoke—it was too enjoyable for words. The glasses drained, May and Rose each untied a nickel from the corner of their handkerchiefs which were pinned to the pockets of their dresses.

I took my nickel from a diminutive purse with "Saratoga" etched across its side.

"Hm!" said Rose. "When did you get that?"

"Mama brought it to me when she and Papa came back from Saratoga where Mama went to reduce."

"I'm not allowed to carry a pocketbook on *Shabbas*," said May, with a self-righteous air.

"I know," I said. "I asked Mama why it was that you and Rose could carry money only if it was tied in a handkerchief, and I was permitted to carry mine in a pocketbook."

"What did your Mama say?"

"She said that was a question that only a rabbi could answer."

We hurried on and only paused once again to gaze into the windows of a shoe store that had just opened. "Look," I said, "there are the same patent leather shoes with the pearl button and cloth uppers that Drucilla Adler wore last week!"

"No wonder," May said. "She's as rich as cream, she can have anything. Look at those ballet slippers! Lucky for us we don't have to do that kind of dancing; it must be terrible on the feet."

"Terrible," we all agreed.

We crossed under the elevated down a street that came abruptly to an end, and we were there. Brooks' Dancing School! We ran up the long flight of red-carpetted stairs and entered the dressing rooms, already filled to overflowing. Girls were unbuttoning their shoes, putting on their slippers, or standing before the mirrors, giving a last pat to their sashes, tied in huge bows at their waists.

As we hurried to check our hats and coats we greeted those who smiled and wanted to be friendly. Some were too stuck-up to give us more than a cold stare, but, fortified by being three together, we just stared back. Quickly we changed, and were just in time to follow the others into the ballroom. What a splendid room it was! Crystal chandeliers glittered and sparkled, reflecting the delicate colors of the dresses and the ribbons. "It looks like a field of flowers," I whispered to Rose.

A whistle blew, we walked cautiously across the floor, waxed and shiny as glass, and took our places. The boys looked nice in velvet pants and Eton jackets, white blouses and shining black pumps, but I was too shy to notice them much.

At one end of the room stood Mr. Brooks, our teacher, an elderly man, elegant in long-tailed black coat, his white hair framing his face. Next to him, tall and angular, was Dolly Webster, his granddaughter. A gentle tap from his wand, and Mr. Brooks called us to attention. "Class begin! First position, second position, third position."

The pianist in the gallery began to play, and we followed obediently, never taking our eyes from the shiny, twinkling pumps of our teacher.

The music changed to a waltz. Mr. Brooks raised one arm, his wrist bent, his fingers delicately poised over his head. "Now," he said, "extend the other arm shoulder high —so! Glide, one, two, three, to the right. Hop, cross the feet—so! Now repeat, to the left: one, two, three—cross."

Some of us stepped to the right when we should have gone to the left, colliding none too gently with our neighbors, but the dancers were hastily maneuvered into the correct direction by Dolly, who darted in and out of the rows just for such emergencies.

"Now," said Mr. Brooks, "to conclude the measure, the boys will bow from the waist, and the girls will make a deep curtsy down to the floor."

How graceful I'm getting, I thought, my knees shakily maintaining the low curtsy. There was a giggle behind me. That's the Aarons girl again, I thought. What's so special about her that she can laugh at others?

The music now became faster, and Mr. Brooks, in his immaculate black coattails and white waistcoat, hopped and skipped lightly as he led us through the intricate steps, which were to emerge some weeks later as the Highland Fling. None of us thought it odd that a white-haired gentleman should be our dancing teacher.

We paused for a minute's rest—then the music started again. It was a gay lilt that we all knew. With arms folded across our chests, we bounded into the Sailors Hornpipe. We became sailors, dancing for joy. We lunged forward to haul in the rigging; now, with one hand shading the eyes, we scanned the seas for a sail.

"Sachey forward," roared Mr. Brooks, "now backward." He gave a hitch to his trousers, as sailors are supposed to do. Then, running forward on our heels, we followed him. With arms upraised we tugged at the imaginary ropes and finished in a triumphant glow.

Mr. Brooks blew his whistle and we scattered to find seats, careful to sit with our own clique, glad for the interval of rest which was now ours, to mop our perspiring faces.

It was now Dolly's turn to perform. We looked at her

adoringly. Her flaming red hair heightened the white pallor of her skin, and she appeared to us quite beautiful. The pianist played the opening bar of her music. "Ah," we whispered, "she is going to do the Skirt Dance." Breathlessly we followed every move as she spread her accordion-pleated skirt, opening and closing it like a fan. Enchanted, we watched her do the famous high kick, her legs flung up like arrows to the right and to the left in dizzy succession, only her blue satin slippers peeping out from the voluminous folds of her dress and petticoats. Now she was doing the back bend. Dolly's brick red hair swept the floor—slowly she raised herself, first her arms, then her bony chest, last her shoulders and head. The music grew tremulous—the dance was nearing the climax. With deliberate slowness she spread her legs for the split. Slowly she sank down, inch by inch, as if rending her body in two. As she touched the floor, she gracefully bent her head until her forehead touched her knee, acknowledging. our tumultous applause. How we clapped and clapped!

Years later the pupils of Brooks' Dancing Class watched Pavlova, Mordkin and a host of others perform miracles in the dance, yet rarely did we recapture the breathless wonder that we once had known, watching Dolly Webster do the split or her famous back bends.

"Take your partners for the Lancers," called Mr. Brooks.

I had been so intent watching Dolly that I had forgotten to provide myself with a partner. "Well, I'll sit it out," I decided. May was dancing with a boy, and Rose with another girl. I watched them. How lovely they looked with their crimply curls, their faces flushed with pleasure.

I noticed others sitting out the dance, a few girls, one or two boys. "That's a nice-looking boy sitting across the room," I thought to myself. He looked at me, but I, always shy, looked away.

I had on the salmon pink dress that I hated. Mama had made it, working night after night, and although it was a copy of one at Best's, I still hated it. I made up my mind I would never wear it again. Salmon pink! I can't abide that color to this day.

The dance was over. Girls were laughing and fanning themselves, but I wasn't hot. May was talking with her partner. Rose was nowhere to be seen.

"Take your partners for the Polka," called Mr. Brooks from the center of the floor.

"What's the matter with you—get up!" I reasoned with myself. "Mama sent you to dancing school to learn to be graceful, to be able to talk to others without getting scared." I kept staring at the floor, embarrassed and miserable.

Someone was standing in front of me, black stockings and pumps, knee pants. I looked up. It was the boy I had admired. "Would you like to dance?" He muttered something more, which I couldn't quite catch. I opened my mouth, hardly knowing what to say. "Yes," I said at last and got to my feet. As we made our way, waiting for the music, he said, "I'm new here; I don't know much about dancing."

"That's all right," I answered. "I'm used to that; my brother Sidney is so absent-minded that when he dances with me he is on my feet most of the time."

"Is your brother here, too?"

"No," I said, "he comes with me only to the soirées."

"Those are the formal dances, aren't they?"

"Yes," I said, "there is one at the end of each month, and they are wonderful."

Wonderful? How could I have said that? I seemed to have forgotten how I hated the soirées, sitting up straight on the small, hard, gold-colored chairs that lined the walls, waiting for some boy to come over and ask me to dance. And always I had to dance with Sidney, awkward, clumsy as a bear. Only when we took our places in the Lancers, or Quadrille was there any change of partners —"Ladies in the center, gentlemen in the center; now change, right and left." But when that was over, I continued my vigil along the sides of the wall or danced with Sidney! How relieved and glad we both were when it came time to go.

Suddenly I thought how different it would be if this boy came to the next soirée. To my astonishment, I heard myself saying, "It would be nice if you would come to the next one."

"Perhaps I will," he said. "At least, I'll try."

When the dance was finished, he led me back to where Rose and May were waiting. He bowed to us, and then, as he was about to leave, he shook my hand and bowed again, directly to me.

When we reached the street, it was quite dark. The Sabbath was over.

"Isn't dancing school wonderful?" I said. "You know, I think it is more wonderful than ever!"

15

SUMMER IN THE CATSKILLS

EPHIE HAD GRADUATED from grammar school in June, and he was ready to enter the shop. Yet Mama hesitated. It was July, and the heat was unbearable. "Ephie's growing too fast," Mama confided to her brother when he came to see her before joining his family for his regular weekend in the Catskills.

"Why don't you let him come with me tomorrow and spend a few weeks with us?" asked Uncle.

"Can I come too?" I asked, unashamed, and breathlessly waited for an answer.

"Why not?" said Uncle, pinching my cheek affectionately.

"I won't hear of it," Mama said quickly. "Belle has enough with her own family, and her nephew Mannie is there, too. That's all she would need with two more of mine; she'd have a regular menagerie."

"What trouble can they be?" insisted Uncle. "Don't

say another word. Let them get their clothes and meet me on the 3:15 tomorrow."

That summer in the Catskills was a delight, the taste and flavor of which I have never forgotten.

How Aunt Belle managed to keep that great brood of youngsters busy and happy never troubled us. It was like a miniature camp, but without counsellors to direct or discipline us. We took it for granted that we were to make our own good times, and we did. There was no tennis, no gardening, not even swimming, for there was only a brook, and that was two miles away. Croquet was the only game of skill that we had, and we played it with feverish intensity. The ground was rocky, sloped down hill, and the grass grew only in straggly tufts, having long sur- rendered to the hot sun and to the tramping of our feet. It really required considerable skill, even for adults, to manoeuver the ball successfully through the wickets.

The house itself stood on a hill, and its yellow painted clapboards looked bare against the sky. Lovely rolling country lay all around us, looking like an enormous patch- quilt of violet, green and yellow. In the distance rose the mountains. Below the house and the sloping fields ran the dirt road, and flanking it on one side was a wooden plank walk which ended in a gully with overhanging trees, ferns, stones and cool moss. Here in the bed of a dried-up brook we set up shop, playing store by the hour. The wooden walk was our counter, and on broad leaves of maple or ferns we set out our wares. Buttercup petals or crushed dandelions served for the indispensable butter; seed pods scraped from the wild wheat stalks and collected into an impressive mound made a very commercial-looking cereal; while pine cones and pine needles and red and green choke cherries were all tastefully arranged to look like merchandise. A scale made of a flat piece of wood and precariously balanced on stones was presided over by the one lucky enough to be the storekeeper; she sat at ease in the shady dell and made change—so many little stones for one big stone. The rest of us had to "buy" and tote our infinitesimal parcels back to the "house," usually in the broiling sun where the "Mama" for the occasion would cook, spank her children and put them to bed.

Early in my stay I undertook to make a pine cushion for the day of my homecoming, but I soon tired of the stripping of pine needles, as my fingers grew blacker and stickier, and the pile of needles, for all my labors, failed to grow larger. It will be much nicer to buy a present, I decided. Accompanied by my brother and as many of the cousins as were permitted to go along, we made our way to the village. There was the general store where you could buy feed for your horse or molasses for your bread, but we had eyes only for the little shops and booths smelling of sweet grass and burnt wood. We deliberated long and painfully before we chose the present that was to be the measure of our love. Birchbark canoes and squaws with their papooses on their backs I discarded as not being suitable. Sweet grass napkin rings were cheap, but not nice enough, and the handkerchief boxes made of sweet grass or birch, too expensive. Having exhausted the patience of every shopkeeper on the street, in desperation I selected a wooden well with a tiny bucket suspended under its roof—and all made of "native wood," we were impressively told. Somehow that "well" never looked quite so nice in our gilded parlor, and it disappeared altogether some months after I was home, together with the bunches of everlasting flowers I had so painstakingly carried with me.

Strangely enough we even forgot about books during those vacation days, for there always was so much to do. Often Mannie and I would be sent to the bakery to get some additional loaves of bread, and it was an errand we eagerly sought. Passing Farmer Grey's home, we hurdled a stone fence and landed in his apple orchard. The low, gnarled branches were easy to climb, and as we bit into the small, unripened fruit, our mouths became puckered and dry. We still hopefully continued to sample the apples until the sight of the farmer and his dog warned us to run.

The sun was warm, the road dusty, but soon we reached the brook which was our real objective. Shoes and stockings were discarded, my skirts rolled around my middle, and we waded in, slipping on the smooth boulders and daring each other to step into the deepest pools. Watching the big, ugly bullfrogs or trying to catch killies as they darted in and out of the rocks, only added to the fun. Suddenly, remembering our errand, we struggled into damp stockings and shoes and started again for the bakery. We arrived there at last and raced up the steps of the porch. The good, sweet smell of cake and bread freshly baked made our mouths water. First we bought our cinnamon buns and ate them with rapture; then came the business of selecting the loaves of bread.

The homeward journey was never as exciting. The buns had been eaten, the brook I only remembered by the unpleasant stickiness of dampened petticoat and dress. We walked slowly and scanned the road for a possible ride. Any conveyance was welcome to us. Sometimes we hitched home on a farmer's wagon with it's load of hay, and it required a good boost from the obliging Mannie before I could land on that dizzy height. Sometimes it was a dairy-cart filled with great galvanized containers of milk. We squeezed in with the driver on the front seat and questioned him at length about how many cows he had and how many horses, when he got up in the morning, and when he went to bed. Later, when we left him, we wondered pityingly how he could live here in the winter when snow covered the lonely fields.

In the house itself we children had very few chores. Perhaps the grown-ups thought it was simpler to have us all out of doors as early as possible. The one thing Aunt Belle insisted on was that each of the girls finish a piece of embroidery by the end of summer. Mine, I remember, consisted of two white muslin pillow shams, to be used to cover the pillows in one of the guest rooms. A curly head was outlined on each, one with eyes wide in surprise, under the caption, "Good Morning"; the other, eyes closed under long, curling lashes, with the pleasing title, "Good Night."

Then came the incident that closed the chapter of this happy visit in the Catskills. We had all been invited to a children's party given by friends of my aunt. Dressed in our best summer frocks, we arrived, and were much impressed by the house, all painted white, set back off the road and guarded by two giant maples. We went over to the barn where we examined the yellow fringe-topped carriage and the little buckboard. We jumped on the sleighs tucked away in far corners. The horses snorted and swished their tails to keep away the flies and we soon went back to the house. Not to be outdone by the grandeur of all those horses and carriages, we described the wonderful rides we had taken.

"We hire a stage when we go for rides," we boasted, "with just such a fringe top as yours, only better, because it is so big the whole family can squeeze into it at one time."

"Did you ever go to the Old Mountain House?" Sylvia asked.

"No, but we've gone to Devil's Kitchen and Deer Park."

Nothing, we assured them, could compare to our trip to the Mountain House. First the stage had rushed downhill so fast that the driver had had to put on his brakes as the wheels rattled and bumped over the stony road. When we had come to the long uphill stretches, we all had to get out and walk, to rest the horses. Then, as we reached the top, what a view met our eyes! You could see seven states, with the Hudson River looking like a silver thread! "It's a wonder the hotel doesn't blow clear off the top of the mountain in a storm!" "I couldn't bear to look down the chasm, it was awful!"

At a call to come to the tea-table our interest in nature's wonders was forgotten. We were soon enjoying cake and tea biscuits with jam and berries with cream. Sitting on his haunches, near his young master, was an enormous St. Bernard dog. We politely listened to stories of Rover's pedigree and exploits, but as we watched his drooling, panting jaws we preferred to admire him at a distance.

The party was over. We were about to leave when we were invited to go upstairs to inspect some special treasure. What it was we were to see, I never had the chance to discover. I was the last one to follow the others and had to pass Rover as he sat watching at the foot of the staircase. Instinctively I hesitated. I didn't like the way he looked at me. I wanted to call someone—instead I smiled weakly, grasped the banister, and started up the stairs. I had gotten half way up when I felt something unbearably sharp tear at my arm. Rover, the magnificent, had resented my going upstairs and had sprung upon me and buried his teeth in my arm. My terrified screams brought everyone hurtling down.

By the time the excitement had subsided, my aunt arrived, and I was hurriedly driven to the country doctor. He looked at the gash in my forearm and talked with Aunt Belle of things I vaguely understood, mad dogs, hydrophobia. Then he spoke to me. "My child, I am going to hurt you, but I am certain you will be a brave little girl, for I must cauterize the wound to prevent it from giving you trouble. Give me your hand, and do not move it . . . so. . . ." It was as if a red-hot iron were applied to my raw and mangled flesh. Between clenched teeth I kept back the scream that was trying to burst forth. I was determined to live up to the good opinion the doctor had of me.

A few days later my aunt was relieved to hear that the dog had been shot by the veterinarian, as the doctor had advised. For the remaining weeks of the summer my brother Ephie wrote my letters for me, telling Mama and Papa how happy and well we were. It was something of a shock, therefore, to my Mama, on meeting us at the dock of the Albany Day Boat, to see my arm in a sling. Then began a round of visits to another doctor, who muttered, "If only the dog had not been shot, we could have examined him to see if he had rabies or not. To be absolutely sure, the Pasteur treatment is advisable." Meanwhile, the wound was healing. I showed no signs of barking or any of the other terrible symptoms Mama had been told to expect, and in the busy life that engulfed everyone, the entire incident was soon forgotten. Only the children who owned Rover never forgave me for the loss of their dog, even when they were grown men and women.

16

THE ARTS

THAT THERE WERE houses nicer than ours
never entered my head until I was taken, as a very little
girl, to visit my cousins who lived in a brownstone house
on Fifty-first Street near the East River. "Don't you
have other people living on the floors upstairs?" I asked.

Sylvia answered a little condescendingly, "No, of
course not."

"You have no idea how nice that is," I insisted. "It
was Mr. Reiss, who lives on our first floor, who gave me
that walking doll; it really walked if you turned that
little crank hidden under her skirts. Besides, it's nice in
other ways. You run upstairs to the other tenants, or
they come down to you."

Sylvia remained unimpressed. "Have you still got the
doll?" she asked.

"Goodness, no! Ben took out the little spring long ago.
He said he wanted to see what made it go—he's always
doing things like that."

Those early visits to my cousins were red-letter days. I used to go, accompanied by *Zadie* (grandfather), and the ride uptown on the Second Avenue elevated train was an adventure in itself. As we stood on the platform at Canal Street, the steam engine came into the station, snorting and puffing, and I cautiously retreated to a safe distance. The train made a perilous curve around Twenty-third Street. I clutched Grandpa's arm and begged him not to lean against the side of the car. I was fearful that even my slight weight, not to mention his, would be enough to cause the train to fall over and plunge onto the houses, the top stories of which we could look into, and seemingly almost touch. By the time we reached Thirty-fourth Street the train had climbed still dizzier heights to permit a shuttle train on a lower set of tracks to take passengers to the Thirty-fourth Street ferry. To look down into the street from that height was indeed frightening. In time I got over those silly fears and began making the trip uptown by myself.

When I was eleven years old, Mama decided that I was ready for improvement. "Look how you sit, all humped over. Sit up straight! And I can't understand a word you're reading—you jumble your words together." I looked up from my book, exasperated at the interruption. She continued, "I talked it over with someone who knows about these things. You need elocution lessons!"

"What do I need them for? Ephie needs them more than I do."

Mama paid no attention to my scowling and went on serenely cutting out another patch for the underwear she was mending. "I know all about Ephie—at least he listens to me. With you, it's just carelessness. Besides," added Mama, "to stand up and recite a piece before the family or even for friends, is a nice accomplishment for a girl." With Mama it was no sooner said than done. She discovered Mrs. Loeb, who lived with her husband and a sister on Beekman Place, only a stone's throw from where my cousins lived. She agreed to teach me at her home Sunday mornings.

That winter, poor, dear Mr. Brooks died, and the dancing school was closed. Again Mama was not to be discouraged. She prevailed upon Dolly Webster to take me on as a private dancing pupil, and by some happy coincidence she, too, lived on Beekman Place. So it was that on Sunday mornings, attired in my best, I was all set to conquer the arts. The rest of the day I was free to visit and play with my cousins.

Promptly at ten-thirty I would run up the steps of the brownstone house with the high stoop, where Dolly lived. The door was opened by a "gray" lady. She was gray all over, her face, her hair, and even her dress. She bolted the heavy door after me as if she thought I might change my mind and leave. "Sit you down in the parlor, and Miss Dolly will be ready in a little while."

The hall was dark. I looked inquisitively up the carpetted staircase which led to some mysterious rooms I had never seen. There was not a sound in the house; even the "gray lady" seemed to walk on shadowy feet. I carefully hung up my coat and poke bonnet on the immense hatrack in the hall and went into the parlor to wait. I smelled the same, dank, close smell that reminded me unpleasantly of something; what, I couldn't quite remember. I sat on a spindly chair, only to get up quickly to continue an exploration begun on previous Sundays. I really didn't mind waiting. The room was enormous, and I enjoyed looking at the old, faded photographs in their walnut frames, the oil paintings in their massive gold and black shadow boxes, and the steel engraving of "Winter" hanging over the mantelpiece.

The room was a treasure house of little things. I touched the jars and bowls of china which sprouted on every table, filled with dried grasses, their soft, feathery leaves drooping mournfully. The what-not, with all its bric-a-brac, and especially the diminutive cups and saucers, engaged my attention. They were pretty, I thought, as I examined them, each cup suspended on its own little stand; and some of them even cracked, I wondered why Dolly prized them so. "My precious antiques," she called them. I felt they couldn't compare with the things in Mama's curio cabinet; the little figures of carved ivory, the tiny lace fan, and the silver and enamel spoons, brightly announcing that they had come from Chicago, San Francisco and other far-away places.

I wandered to the other end of the room, picked up a large, heavily bound book from the table and settled myself in one of the big armchairs. The title, *Dante's Inferno*, meant nothing to me, and I began to turn the pages. Purgatory—Hell. Devils leaped from the pages and horned creatures with long sharp forks were prodding miserable, terrified human beings who writhed in their agony trying to escape the flames. Other devils were heaping coals upon the fires and tongues of flame enveloped the struggling snake-like figures. I looked up in terror. What a relief to see Dolly standing next to me! I hadn't even heard her come into the room. She smiled her wan smile and gave me her limp hand as I struggled to my feet, still holding onto the book.

"Is there such a place as—" I hesitated over the word.

"Hell?" Dolly finished the sentence for me. "When I was a child I believed there was," she said. "Our preacher talked of it as if he had been there and knew it intimately. Some people have to be frightened into being good. But some day you will read Dante for pleasure. It's a classic."

I shook my head. "Never for pleasure," I emphatically replied.

Together we cleared a large space near the big square piano, and began the lesson. I followed Dolly's every move; her grace and effortless dancing I admired more than ever. She sat down to the piano while I danced alone, and she nodded her head in time to the music.

"Now," she said, after I had rested for a few minutes, "Let us try something quite new and daring. It's a scarf dance. You think of a story and interpret it by your steps and the movement of the scarves. To begin, try to follow me."

Soon we were both whirling about in a maze of pastel-colored chiffon. Then, pausing as if arrested in her flight, Dolly, with a great sweep of her arms, wound the scarves about her. "She looks like a huge tiger lily," I thought as I glimpsed the flaming red of her hair emerging from the folds of chiffon. Then she deftly unwound them and started leaping once again. As I followed her blindly, trying to capture the pattern of her dance, my legs became entangled in the silky web. I stumbled and fell. The what-not with its bric-a-brac shook and swayed, then righted itself. After Dolly extricated me from the entangling chiffons, she went over and lovingly fingered her cups and saucers.

"Some were my mother's and some belonged to my grandmother," she said. "I'm glad nothing happened to them."

"And that dance we were doing," I managed to pant, "what was it supposed to mean?"

"Couldn't you guess?" she asked. "It was a lover beckoning to her beloved, and then both trying to escape the vengeance of the pursuers."

"Oh," I said. "I had it all figured out that we were doing a story from Dante's *Inferno*. Even Dolly laughed then.

As she followed me into the hall where I put on my hat and coat, she said, "Next week we will try something less violent; it will be safer."

Again I held her limp, slightly moist hand, in a gesture of farewell.

A quick run down the steps, and a few minutes later I was mounting the steps of another brownstone house as like the first as two peas in a pod. Mrs. Loeb, my elocution teacher, opened the door herself as if she had been waiting for me. She was a tall, heavily built woman, and her rich, melodious voice boomed as she led the way downstairs to the basement dining-room.

"Here," she said, "our voices will disturb no one."

She sat down heavily in the only armchair, while I took off my hat and coat. The warm sunshine was coming through the iron railings of the basement windows and showed up in all its plainness the golden oak table, the tall, straight chairs standing guardian around it, and the crystal closet, filled with glass and china.

"As you are rather late this morning, we won't have time to review any of your pieces, but we will make up for it next time. Suppose you start with the very last thing I gave you," and with a smile, she nodded for me to begin.

Thinking to make amends for my tardiness, and thus to make up for lost time, I started in a nice, racy tempo.

> "Stay, jailor, stay, and hear my woe!
> She is not mad who kneels to thee."

Mrs. Loeb held up an imperious hand. "Stop. Go no further. You did not announce the title, or the author! And look at your posture! Stand up straight. No, not the stomach, the chest should be thrust forward!" Vainly I tried to imitate the movement of her ample bosom.

"So—that is better. Now begin again."

> *The Maniac*, by Mathew Lewis—
> "Stay, jailor, stay, and hear my woe!
> She is not mad who kneels to thee;
> I'll rave no more in proud despair;
> My language shall be mild, though sad,
> But yet I firmly swear, I am not mad, I am not . . ."

Once more my teacher held up her hand to stay my impetuous flow. "And why did you not kneel? Do not the lines say, 'She is not mad who kneels to thee?' Let me show you," and she struggled out of her chair. Her smiling face took on a look of sadness. Her hands were raised in piteous plea. She was on her knees, and I scarcely noticed the cracking sound of her joints until she had started to rise again.

"You see what I mean?" She gave me an encouraging smile to continue. I went on with the sorrowful tale until I neared the end.

> "O Hark what mean those yells and cries?
> His chain some furious madman breaks;
> He comes—I see his glaring eyes:
> Now, now, my dungeon gate he shakes.
> Help! Help! He's gone! O fearful . . ."

"Louder, louder," boomed Mrs. Loeb, again rising from her chair. "Open your mouth wide, let the words come out, enunciate clearly, as if you were in a vast auditorium. Start from the cry, 'Help! Help!'" And like a duet, my teacher accompanied me until I ended on that last, wild shriek—

> "Help! Help! He's gone! O fearful woe!
> Such screams to hear, such sights to see!
> My brain, my brain, ah laugh ye fiends;
> Your task is done—I'm mad—I'm mad!"

A strange voice interrupted us. "Sure, ma'am, is nothin' amiss?"

We both turned, and in the doorway stood Nora, the maid, her arms full of table linen, and a look of alarm on her face.

"What is it?" my teacher fairly hissed, for like a true artist, she hated to be disturbed.

"Sure, I thought—well, it's no matter." Whatever it was, Nora had decided to keep it to herself. She went on, "Beggin' your pardon, but your sister told me to remind you that it's time for me to be layin' the table for dinner, that it's my Sunday off, that Mr. Loeb is hungry, and that the roast will be ruined!"

"Take the roast out of the oven, Nora, and you will be able to come in here in a very few minutes." Mrs. Loeb turned to me again.

"Let me see, where was I? Oh, yes, that last was very much better. You must learn to speak with utter abandon. In a few more lessons, it will be perfect."

"Oh, couldn't I have something funny for the next lesson?" I asked. "Of course, I like 'The Maniac,' but for that party, you remember, you promised me—"

"Yes, yes, my dear, I haven't forgotten. I have the very thing for you. I have it all written out. It is called 'Sister's Beaux,' a little number I wrote myself. Have you any older sisters?" she asked me suddenly.

"No, but I have several—"

"Too bad," she broke in. "However, most people have, unfortunately, and they will love it—the piece, I mean the things that happen. Memorize it for next time. Of course, if you had an older sister—" Mrs. Loeb broke off and suddenly looked into space. I wondered if that plump little woman who sometimes sat through my lesson, could have been such an older sister.

"I'll do my best to learn it for next week," I said as I started to put on my hat and coat.

The savory smells from the kitchen now filled the room, and I realized suddenly that I was very hungry.

"To sum it all up in a nutshell," Mrs. Loeb went on, as she accompanied me through the dark hallway to the gate, "Remember Mr. Shakespeare's famous lines, 'Suit the action to the word, and the word to the action!'"

I sped through the basement gate and ran the short block that separated me from the Fifty-first Street house.

17

A SUNDAY AFTERNOON

I WAS just in time. I was warmly greeted by everyone, and after kissing my aunt and uncle, took my seat between the two older girls, Sylvia and Mabel. "How do you feel today, Aunt Belle?" I dutifully inquired.

In spite of the fact that Aunt Belle looked extremely robust as well as very beautiful, she seemed to expect a tender solicitude on the part of every member of the family. I never asked Mama how she felt; we just took her good health and strength for granted.

Uncle sat at the head of the table, Aunt next to him. Anyone could see that they adored each other. Uncle always addressed her as "My Love," and his hands, when not engaged in eating or cutting up the food for the younger children, would be lovingly patting hers. The girls never interrupted, no matter how tiresome the talk of the grown-ups became, and they never asked to leave the table before the meal was over. I thought, it was all very "genteel," an idea I had culled from my recent reading.

"Will anyone have more chicken?"

I looked up quickly as my Aunt spoke. There were some polite murmurs of "No, thank you," and I swallowed the "*I* will," which was so nearly on my lips.

It was a lovely dinner, the girls so well behaved, and the service so orderly. Yet I missed the noisy argument of our own table at home. Besides, Mama would have thought we were ill if we did not pass our plates for at least two helpings!

We were now waiting for the dessert. Uncle carefully wiped the silky fringe of his drooping mustache after every course, a performance that fascinated me. He cleared his throat. "My love," Uncle began, as he again patted Aunt's plump, little hand, "I am afraid the girls have been very negligent in their studies this past week. Sylvia's marks in school—" He shook his head and glanced sadly at the culprit. "Even Mr. Pereira who makes such an effort to come here on Sundays mornings to teach you your Bible and Hebrew—even he is disappointed."

His eyes now rested on Mabel. "As for you, my dear, I expected something—" He never got the chance to finish. Mabel's lips quivered; she was thin as a broomstick and in delicate health. Mabel looked up wanly. "I think," she whispered weakly, "I am getting a pain in my stomach." None knew better than Mabel how to divert attention from any unpleasant subject. Uncle sighed. Aunt Belle came to the rescue of her fledglings. "Isie, my love, you worry the children; I'm sure they do better than most others."

Uncle, who would have liked a family of geniuses, or at least of brilliant scholars, was forced to capitulate. He sighed again, patted Aunt's hand, and said, "All right, my Love; it can wait. I will go over their homework with them tonight."

To change the subject, Aunt inquired, "How was the meeting at the hospital this morning?" Uncle brightened up visibly. "After all," he murmured, as if to himself, "there are other worlds to conquer, and the children will no doubt learn in time; they are still so young."

"The meeting? It came off better than I hoped. There were, of course, some difficult moments, when Mr. Wallach and Mr. Strauss presented their point of view—something about 'oil and water,' that the German Jews and the recent immigrants who came from Poland and Russia would not mix, even in charitable work. But Jacob Schiff quickly put an end to all such talk. He's a man! A man of whom we can be proud. He told them, 'Some of us who came from Germany have had advantages they lack. Give them time.' Then he turned to me, to *me*, Bella. 'You can help us,' he said. 'You are Russian-born, and you know them and understand us. You have worked with us, you believe in our desire to be of service to our beloved America, which has taken us to her bosom.' I don't know why he thinks I can be so helpful," and Uncle gave a deprecating little smile.

"Because he knows your worth," said Aunt lovingly.

The dessert was eaten in an atmosphere of renewed cheer. A quick grace terminated the meal.

"Thank goodness it's a short one," Doris whispered to me as she joined in the "We thank you, Heavenly Father, for the bread we have eaten." Soon we were scrambling for our hats and coats to go out of doors.

The street was quiet. There seemed to be few other children on the block, and for a while we were content to walk up and down, arm in arm. But not for long. A few doors beyond the house was the East River, and a low stone wall, surmounted by a tall, iron-spiked fence, shut off the steps that led down to the water's edge. The river drew us like a magnet. We walked along the ledge, grasping the rail, and watched the tugboats lazily push the scows. Blackwell's Island lay before us; the buildings shorn of their summer foliage looked stark in the brightness of the winter sun.

"I can see them running about," I announced triumphantly.

"See whom?" my cousins asked, eagerly scanning the water.

"The prisoners, in their striped uniforms."

I became expansive, feeling myself somehow challenged. "Sometimes they escape—it's not so difficult as you think." Then I added in a shivery voice, "When it's dark, they creep close to the water's edge, take off their prison clothes and swim in the icy current to this side of the river. Perhaps they reach this spot, right beneath us. There a friend lies hidden, waiting with clothes to help them escape."

Doris looked up, her pretty face in a grimace preparatory to crying. "Please don't speak of such things,"

whispered Sylvia. "She won't be able to sleep tonight."
She put a protecting arm around her little sister. "Let's
play a game—how about button-button? Or suppose we
play puss-in-the-corner in our backyard?"

Being the oldest, I volunteered to be "It" and hurried
ahead of them. The summer house in the corner yard
caught my attention. I kept staring at it. Was it only a
few months ago that it had been a *Succah*, a glowing
symbol of the harvest festival? Now it looked forlorn, not
even tempting us as a playhouse. The glass-covered roof,
now thick with dust had been removed for the *Succoth*
festival. In its place sweet-smelling boughs of bayberry
lay in thick layers on the wooden slats, through which the
sky peeped, and through which, alas, the rain also poured.
Inside the *Succah* there had hung suspended from the
boughs, festoons of cranberries, corn in their husks, green
and red peppers, carrots, squash, green and purple
grapes. How beautiful it had looked! How glad I had
been when Aunt Belle made Mama promise we would stay
for supper, as I had never before eaten a meal in a
Succah. The riot of autumn color overhead, the gleaming
silver and crystal on the table had made it look gay and
festive.

Uncle sang the blessing over the wine, then over the
bread—passing to each of us a piece of the *challa* and
the cup for a sip of the wine. The maid served the soup,
and little clouds of steam rose from the huge soup tureen.
But neither the soup nor my jacket warmed me; even
the candles were blowing in the wind. I sneezed. Mama
stopped in the middle of a sentence to say *"Gesundheit,"*
which was piously repeated by Aunt and Uncle.

"I agree with you, Belle," Mama went on, "a Young Women's Hebrew Association would be a wonderful thing."

I sneezed again and again. Mama furtively put her hand to my head. She forgot the philanthropic dream that until now had engaged her attention. She rose from the table. "You'll have to excuse me, Belle, but I can't wait for the rest of the dinner. I completely forgot that Hannah and Rachel Mayers are coming to our house tonight. We'll have to leave right away."

I protested loudly, that I wanted to stay, but it was of no use. Uncle saw us out to the gate, and Mama spoke her mind more freely. "A *Succah* truly is a beautiful thing, but it is enough to go into it for a few minutes, for the *Kiddush*, to recall the days of wandering in the wilderness. But to sit in the cold and wet after three days of rain, believe me, is tempting Providence! After all, this is October, not July, and we are in New York, not Palestine! Take my advice, Belle is still delicate," and with that the gate slammed behind us.

"Puss—puss—aren't you going to play?" the cousins shouted at me. "Sophie, what are you staring at—stop dreaming!"

"I'm tired," I pleaded, suddenly recalled to the present, "let us go into the house."

We raced up to the third floor, to Sylvia's and Mabel's room, and stopped in to see their invalid grandmother, Aunt Belle's mother, whose room adjoined their own. Unable to walk, she was, nevertheless, a rather awesome figure, dressed in her black silk, a lace cap with a purple

ribbon on her head, which never stopped shaking even for a minute.

"What makes her head shake like that?" I had asked the first time I had seen her.

"It's her sickness," Sylvia told me confidentially. Now I was used to it too.

Mabel and the others went over and kissed the dark, gaunt face, and lovingly touched the stiffened hands. Then we all left her as suddenly as we had come.

Once again we went tumbling down the stairs and made a noisy entrance into the nursery. There was Lillian, aged two, sitting sedately on the rug, playing with her toys and looking for all the world, like one of the golden-haired cherubs on our parlor ceiling. But most of all, we admired the new baby.

"Hush, hush," admonished Aunt Belle from the couch.

We tiptoed over to the bassinet, a mass of lace and ribbons. "Isn't he cute?" "Did you ever see anything so adorable?" chirped the cousins.

"It must be nice to have a boy at last, after four girls I said to my aunt believing I was being extremely tactful. "Not at all," said my aunt, as she smiled at her little girls. "We think girls are even nicer in some ways, but they are happy to have a little brother."

Again we went tearing down the stairs to the kitchen, where Delia and the cook, now rested from their labors, had hot cocoa and buns waiting for us. I looked at the clock; it was almost time for me to go.

"Sure, now" said Delia, turning to me, "aren't you goin' to do that Irish piece before you leave? I loved that last thing yer did about a Dutchman, but I'm keen on hearin' the Irish thing yer promised us." I required no further urging.

I stood up in the middle of the kitchen and cheerfully gave samples of my recently acquired "art" before an admiring, if not too discriminating, audience.

Occasionally I stayed overnight with my cousins. At such times, I would be startled out of my sleep, as a tall figure, clad only in his night shirt, tiptoed into the room, adjusted the covers, and quietly left the room again.

In our house, it was Mama who made these nocturnal rounds, only her bare feet and her long white night-gown visible in the dimness. Mama and Uncle were brother and sister; that seemed to explain everything.

18

COBBLESTONES AND UNIONS

FOR MONTHS the roadbed of East Broadway had been torn up, the city having finally seen the need of relaying it. What this had to do with the current New York City politics was not quite clear to me, though there were many sarcastic and cynical remarks made by the grown-ups that "the work would be sure to be coming along, now that Election Day was not far off."

The white granite blocks, each as large as a shoe box, stacked five feet high, provided a new outlet for the energies and ingenuity of all of us children in the neighborhood. Michael, the policeman on our beat, for whom we all had great affection, warned us to be cautious, as children often came to school limping and bruised.

I asked him, "Michael, why do they call these stones cobblestones?"

" 'Tis easy to see you are city bred. It's for the horses' hooves that the stones of the streets, just like the feet of the horses, must be cobbled. It's the iron horseshoes,

which fit the rounded tops of the stones, that keep the
galloping horses from slippin' all over the place."

"Thank you, Michael," I answered, not very sure that
I understood just what he meant.

Glad to talk of something else, I said, "Michael, Mama
is always telling me to inquire about Mary."

"Aw, 'tis fine she is, and tell your Ma that it won't
be long now."

"But what is it that won't be long now?" I asked. "It's
the blessed event that's soon comin'. Run along now, and
look careful crossing the heap of cobbles."

No matter how much we had to do after school, we
would stand and watch the laborers lay the street, stone
by stone. One group of workers would pound them down
with iron sledge hammers, and another group would come
up with buckets of steaming hot tar, which they would
pour into each crevice until only the white tops remained.

I rarely ventured into the narrow streets adjacent to
our own. Perhaps the tenements of Ludlow, Essex and
Hester Streets, with their overhanging fire-cocapes,
looked forbidding to me. Thousands of people lived there
under conditions I did not begin to understand. The
sidewalks were almost impassable. For every neighborhood store, dozens of pushcarts lined the curb, tended by
old men and women draped in fantastic shawls and over-
coats. Loudly and vociferously, in Yiddish and broken
English, they chanted their wares. "Lemons, onions,
matjes herring that will melt in your mouth, *lebidig*
(live) fish." Indeed, the fish were still alive as they flopped
and pulsated in their baskets.

Sometimes I went with Mama on a hurried trip to

the market. There were some who counted on her weekly trade. One, especially. Rifke, a widow, whom Mama had set up in business. There she stood next to her stand, never calling or hawking as the others did, and no admonishing on Mama's part could change her.

"Mama," I asked, "why does Rifke just stand there? She'll never sell anything if she doesn't call out like everyone else." Mama pursed her lips, annoyed at her protege. "She can't forget she's the daughter of a rabbi. But people buy—she won't starve."

While Mama was busy, I investigated wares of a different kind. At first, I was tempted by the pungent-smelling pickels swimming in a barrel of brine, but instead selected a huge pretzel, thickly sprinkled with coarse salt, which with dozens more hung at one end of the apple woman's cart.

One winter afternoon, after school, and despite falling snow and icy sidewalks, I started out for a store on Delancey Street, bent on acquiring one of those new shiny pencil boxes of lacquered wood that other girls in my class owned. A gust of wind-driven snow pushed me violently towards the curb. I tried to clutch the lamppost, but slipped and fell headlong into the slush and snow of the gutter. My books scattered in every direction. I tried to get up, but the pain in my ankle was so intense that I groaned out loud. I got to my knees and crawled nearer the curb. No one paid attention to me; everyone was hurrying away from the markets, as it was Friday afternoon, and the Sabbath not many hours off.

Suddenly I heard something that made me look up quickly. My heart almost stopped beating. A truck driver was yelling at his horse who was out of control and was almost upon me. With a horrified shriek I grabbed the hands of a passerby, who at that very moment had seen my danger and reached me just in time. I was crying hysterically. A crowd gathered around us. "*Nu, Nu*," said the giant who had rescued me, "What are you crying about? You're all right, kid, nothing happened."

"Something is wrong with my leg," I managed to stutter. "It hurts me so here, at the ankle."

He shook his head sympathetically, as he held me by the arm and spoke to a man who was with him. "Here, Jan, come here, hold her up for a minute." He took hold of my ankle and gave it a quick, sharp pull. I let out another shriek, but immediately afterward I felt better. I looked at him, reassured, and tried standing alone.

"Now," he cautioned, "stamp your foot down—so—give it a good kick." He illustrated these instructions with kicks and stampings, which I feebly tried to imitate. "Well, kid, guess you're all right now, eh? Where do you live, far from here?" I said that I lived at 251 East Broadway.

"Good. Then you haven't many blocks to go."

"I know my Mama would want to thank you for what you have done," I began bashfully and started limping in the direction of home.

"Look, Jan, maybe we better see the kid gets home all right, it will only take us a few blocks out of our way."

I walked between them and leaned on their arms for support, and we were soon talking like old friends.

"And what is your Mama's and Papa's name?"

When I told him he laughed rather gruffly. "You mean your Mama and Papa are in the shirt business?"

I nodded my head, and he gave his companion a nudge that almost sent him off his balance. "To think I should be doing a favor for such a *momser* (bastard)— You've got a couple of brothers, too, eh?"

"I've got a lot of brothers," I said proudly.

"Yes, we know them. Eh, Jan?"

"Yeah," said Jan. "We know them."

As we turned into East Broadway and reached our corner, I saw Mama standing near our stoop, talking to a group of people who were crowded around her.

"Mama," I cried. "Mama!" My call was almost a scream.

She turned, hurried towards me, and I could no longer keep back my tears.

"My darling, what's happened? Who hurt you?"

"It's my foot, Mama. I was nearly run over. If it had not been for these two—"

"Nearly run over, Oh, my God!"

As Mama looked up, she recognized my rescuers, but in no kindly spirit. Holding me close to her, she faced my two friends in a frenzy of anger. "What have you done to my child? Cowards, good-for-nothings, Cossacks —and you call yourselves labor leaders! I'll teach you a lesson; I'll have you in jail for this!"

"But, Mama," I cried to her unheeding ears, "Mama, they saved me, they didn't hurt me."

But Mama was not in any mood to listen. "Charlie, go get a policeman."

Charlie was the foreman in the cutting department and

devoted to the family. Before he could even answer, Jan reached out and grabbed him by the collar and shook him as a cat might shake a mouse. "You dirty scab," he said. By this time the crowd had grown, and there were angry cries and threats. Suddenly I saw my brother Abe without hat or coat, making his way towards us and urging Mama to go into the house. To this I added my own cries of pain and anguish.

As Mama finally turned, and we descended the few steps to our basement, I heard the voice of Michael, the policeman, "Come now, break it up, break it up, I say! Come on now. If you've no business here, get moving— Come now, or I'll have to send for the wagon."

A few moments later I was lying on the leather sofa in the dining room. Bessie, our new girl, was sent to fetch a basin with chunks of ice and towels. As Mama was putting on the cold compress to my swollen ankle, Bessie kept on talking, never stopping to catch her breath. "Aw, now, did you ever see the like of that? What were they trying to do, kidnap you, was it? And it is a good thing they didn't murder you entirely!"

"Bessie," said Mama, "stop jabbering." Sitting down next to me, she said. "Tell me, how did this thing happen, tell me everything."

This was the moment for which I had been waiting. I described my fall, how I saw the horse of the brewery truck coming towards me, his hooves almost over my head. "And then, Mama, just as I screamed, there were *his* hands, pulling me out of danger." Bessie kept up a running commentary with "Bless you, now," or "You can thank the angels above and the blessed saints."

Just as I finished Papa came into the room with Abe and Harry, and followed by the two men whom I looked upon as my heroes. "Fannie," said Papa, "here are Barney Hillman and Jan Pulski, the delegates who are causing all the trouble downtown. They want to talk with us. It won't take long. I see the table is set already for *Shabbus*. Is it all right for us to sit here?"

"Why not?" said Mama—"Only no excitement; we've had enough for one day," and she pointed to me, lying in state on the leather couch.

"Mama," Harry began, "I want to tell you that Barney and Jan had nothing to do with her falling in the—"

"Yes, yes, I know! It's lucky for them. It's a lucky thing they didn't—"

"But, Mama—" I said.

"You keep quiet and stay quiet until the doctor comes."

"*Nu*," said my father, "we didn't come here to *schmoos* about the child, and thank God she'll be all right, too. Sit down everyone, and let us make it short and quick. Now, about wages. You admit we pay more than our competitors, as much as you are demanding, yes? And the factory is good; it's light and clean. And what's more, in my shop a man gets a chance to rise, to be somebody, not a cog in the machine. Many a man who runs his own business today got his start under me. You know that I speak the truth. Now, what do you want of me?"

"You know well enough what we want of you. We want to organize a union, and that goes for the whole trade."

"Look, Papa," said my brother Harry in a conciliatory tone, "maybe—"

"No," said Papa, "I'm not looking. A union! I won't have a union in my shop as long as I live. In America a man is free to come and go, to work, to make his living, and if he is not afraid to work, if he is honest and not a crook, he will make a good life for himself and his family. What's mine, I made by the sweat of my brow. That's what I believe in. If it's a union you want, to dictate to me and my wife whom to hire and whom to fire, I tell you, you won't get it, that's final."

"Come, Barney," said Jan, "let's get out of here." They took their hats and coats. At the door Barney turned, looking Papa straight in the eye. "Let me tell you this, big Boss," he said, "if it's war you want, you'll get it—if it's scabs you think you'll get, I'm telling you, don't try it. That's one thing we won't stand for, not from you or the poor slobs that want to risk their lives for the few extra pennies. A strike you'll have, not because we've got anything against you or the Missus, but because of the workers who are in the sweatshops on starvation wages for ten hours a days and are slaves begging for their miserable jobs. You call that free competition, democracy, the land of golden opportunity. *Pfui* upon such democracy! I call it *dog eat dog*, that's what it is. War you want, so you'll get it!"

Abe took them to the door. The iron gate slammed upon them.

Mama roused herself as if she had been thinking deeply. "If every manufacturer, Simon, and by that I mean everyone, would raise the wages and fix the hours the way the union wants, who knows, maybe a union wouldn't be as terrible as we fear. Besides, if the whole trade has the same headache, what have we to lose?"

"Never," blustered Papa, but it seemed to me he was now less sure of himself.

"All I say," continued Mama, "don't let's be hasty. Go upstairs now and wash up. Let the boys go up, too; it's almost time to *bench licht* (bless the Sabbath candles)."

A half hour later, we took our accustomed places at the table. My foot had been tightly bandaged by the doctor who had come and gone, and this permitted me to sit with the family, my foot raised on a stool.

Everything shone with Sabbath brightness. The candles cast a soft glow over the white cloth that still concealed the two braided *challas*. The peace of the Sabbath had descended upon our home. Papa stood at the head of the table, his head covered with a skull cap, a glass of wine in his hand. He intoned the *Kiddush* in a soft, musical Hebrew, a chant we all knew and loved. *"Boruch atto Adonai,* Blessed art thou, Oh Lord, King of the Universe—"

Suddenly, there was a crash of shattered glass and a terrifying thud as a great cobblestone struck the iron grating of our basement window.

I burst out, "It can't be Jan. Oh, I know it can't be Jan or Barney!"

"Of course not, you little fool," answered Abe, "it's the Henry Street gang. That's their way of saying *Good Shabbus.*"

19

THE STRIKE

A FEW DAYS LATER, coming home from school, I found my older brothers, and Mama and Papa, sitting around the table. Surprised at this unusual manner of spending a working day, I called out, "Is today some sort of holiday I forgot?"

Mama looked at me and said drily, "Yes, it's a holiday that's not in the *louach* (religious calendar). The shop is on strike!"

So Jan Pulski had kept his threat.

"Only our shop, Mama?" I asked.

"No, everyone. The whole needle trade is at a standstill. If you go into the kitchen, you'll find some cocoa on the stove. Then go up and practice like a good girl. If you wait until Sidney comes home, he'll want to practice, and you'll fight as usual. In the end neither of you will practice."

"I will, Mama, in just a little while. I have to draw something with my compass before I forget how to do it."

It wasn't really the drawing that kept me dawdling in my corner of the table. I had to know about the strike. They were discussing it, "mapping out their strategy," Abe called it.

"How many can we depend on to stick to us?"

"The real problem is to keep the cutting room going —how, otherwise, can we get enough bundles to the out-of-town factories?"

Papa strode up and down the room, shaking his head belligerently. "We'll see who can hold out longer, they or us."

Weeks passed, and the strike dragged on. There seemed to be no end in sight.

"Who can keep this up?" Mama complained bitterly, night after night, as she waited for Papa and the boys to come home, often guarded by a policeman. "We'll lose our business. What sense does it all make?" She shrugged her shoulders. "And the workers—God knows, if by this time they have even bread to eat!"

Each day Mama was full of hope that a settlement would be reached, only to hear the same disappointing news at night. She vented her wrath on the union organizers. "Those walking delegates, they don't want to settle. Recognize the union, that's what they want, so that they can dictate to us."

Mama had not gone to the shop for weeks. Her girls dropped in almost daily and asked to be allowed to go to work. "For you," they said, "we'll gladly go through fire."

Mama was touched and proud of their love, but she would not hear of it. "Besides," Mama confided one day to Lizzie, one of the foreladies, "we may soon give up the ladies' underwear department." Mama quickly answered the look on Lizzie's face. "You don't have to worry, nor the other girls, either. If we can't place everybody in our own shop, Jake Goldberg would kiss his ten fingers to get any of our operators. I don't have to praise myself, but you know how he feels about the girls I have trained."

That night while Papa was trying to forget his troubles in the pages of his newspaper, Mama further elaborated her ideas. She was combing my hair, while I sat on a wooden chair before her, my head still aching from the vigorous rubbing it had received.

"You know, Simon, I haven't patience anymore with the embroideries, the petticoats with their flounces, the muslin drawers, open and and closed, the chemises down to the knees. Take my word for it, a change is coming in the ladies' underwear trade, as I told you before, not once, but twenty times. I'm thinking of closing the department for good. When the strike is over, we'll make room for something new—maybe a line of pajamas, men's nightgowns are not selling the way they used to either."

"Ouch," I cried out, almost jerking the comb out of Mama's hand, while my wet hair flapped uncomfortably about my face. "You hurt me!"

"That's because you don't hold your head still. I have to take the knots and tangles out before I can use the fine comb."

This ritual was performed religiously, and no excuse of mine ever succeeded in inducing Mama to postpone it. Tonight had been no exception. To my excuse and plea that I was too tired, Mama had replied, "No, tonight and not tomorrow night."

"As I was saying, Simon," Mama went on, paying no more attention to my complaints, "we'll stop making the women's underwear and make room for something new. In business you have to go backward or forward, you can't stand still."

Papa put down his newspaper. "If you ask me, the business is already going backward. To listen to you, no one would imagine that we are going through one of the worst strikes we ever had—and you talk of opening a new department."

"Believe me, *I* could settle the strike! I didn't like to say anything at the manufacturers' meeting the other night, especially with all those *Daitchen* present (a reference to the older, more cultured German element, who together with certain Gentile firms, represented the top-notchers in the industry). A woman isn't supposed to know anything about business, or dare open her mouth. But I could tell them a thing or two. So the factories would work nine hours instead of ten. Nine hours a day, six days a week, is enough, if only a man wants to work."

"And the piece-workers—what about them?" Papa asked.

"A little increase wouldn't hurt there either. The boss has nothing to lose. You pay those who produce and not the schlemiels who fall asleep over their work or run every minute to the water-closet." With comb upraised, she halted Papa's exclamation of impatience. "They'll have to raise the pressers and the folders. I've seen myself a man cannot raise a family on ten or eleven dollars a week.

Give them a dollar raise, and they won't listen to those agitators and walking delegates."

"Am I at last allowed to get in a word?" asked Papa impatiently. Thank you! There you stand in judgment like another King Solomon. Raise wages, shorten hours! Figure your wages, mine, Abe's, Harry's. I'm not counting Ephie's; he's only a beginner. But what about the investment on our capital? Aren't we entitled to some return on our investment? Money that we made, slaving for years, night and day. You know that every dollar we could spare we put back into the business for machines or another factory. Now, when we could produce, they go on strike!"

"That's exactly what I am trying to figure out," Mama answered quietly. "With all our work, why don't we make more money? Something is wrong somewhere. We can't raise the price of our shirts, our competitors would under-sell us. But you know who are our worst enemies? Fair competition one can meet. But those contractors who get shirts made in the tenements, the sweatshops—they are our real enemies, and the enemies of the working man, too. Who can compete with them? If I could figure how to save on the cloth, maybe use only a few inches less on every shirt—"

"Mama," I exclaimed. "I still have to finish my homework, and my back hurts from sitting so long."

"All right, you're all through. Put this dry towel around your head so you don't catch cold."

Mama picked up her sewing. "Tell me, Simon, does it say anything about the strike in the newspapers?"

"Nothing new, except that more and more are going back to work, just as I expected."

"Who was down today?"

"The same handful. Today it was Abraham and Sam Isaacs who nearly had their heads broken. I don't know what they want of us. Have I ever refused a man work, no matter how green he was? And I kept them, too, when the season was slack. Some are *frum* (pious), but you know as well as I, some are not. It isn't enough for them that the shop is closed on *Shabbus*, but just try to keep them a minute after half past three on Friday! You'd think they were *rovs* or *zaddicks* (saints)! Our profit is reckoned in pennies on every shirt, and they expect me to perform miracles."

I listened hard to every word. It wasn't only that I had been watching Mama these last weeks as she waited for Papa and the boys to come home, night after night, and whispered, "Thank God, they're home safe." No, it wasn't that alone that made me want to cry out and tell Mama, that I was to Amy's house the other night. Her married sister was there, her husband worked in one of the shops that are on strike. They were suffering. She said that she had begged her husband to go back to his job, but he had refused to go and be a scab. When Amy's mother told her sister my name, she spat in my face and left the house. Amy cried and I cried.

"What's a scab, Amy?" I asked.

Amy didn't know either, but her mother said, "You know, my child, it is not good when working people do not stand together. If things in the trade are so bad that workers bring themselves to strike, how shameful it is for another worker to take his place. Such is a scab, my child. We do not blame your Mama and Papa—they alone cannot change anything."

Now, as I was listening to Papa and Mama I felt I had to speak out. "Mama," I began, but the words stuck in my throat. I was afraid of Papa's temper. I could just imagine what he would say: "You, an eleven-year-old nobody, who knows only how to waste her time learning to recite pieces and go to dancing school, you're going to give me advice on labor troubles!"

Mama's voice brought me back to reality. "Look, there you sit dreaming, with your mouth wide open as if you were making speeches to yourself. Go to bed. Be sure you don't open any windows, and keep the towel on your head. Your hair is still damp."

On Saturday night Uncle Israel came to see us. He, too, felt the need to talk things over. He sat next to my brother Harry, whom he loved very much. "He'll be the future head of the business one day," he once told Mama, at which she made believe she was very angry.

Uncle was talking in his soft, quiet manner, and everyone listened respectfully. "It's no use. The industry cannot afford to raise wages, not at the price they get for their merchandise. As for the closed shop, and to allow them to form a union, that is absolutely out of the question."

"But, Uncle," I piped up before I realized what I was saying, "if people who own factories can have an association, why can't those who work in them have one, too?"

Papa glared at me, too surprised to say anything. Mama gave me one of her "looks," but she said, without raising her voice, "Does she know what she's talking about? She was sitting in someone's house and they filled her ears with a lot of nonsense."

Uncle shook his head solemnly and said, "Children should be seen, but not heard."

"I don't know why she's allowed to be here altogether," blustered Abe.

"Ssh-Ssh, the parlor is too lonely, and the children are sleeping in the other rooms," Mama quickly answered him.

Harry had hardly noticed my excursion into the realm of labor problems, so occupied was he with his own thoughts. "If we could step up production or reduce other costs, an increase in wages wouldn't be impossible," he said.

Mama beamed. "God bless my Harry. Those were my very thoughts. I told your father only the other day that if a shirt could be cut, not so full, so that—"

"Fannie," Papa interrupted, a little anxiously, I thought, "Israel is not interested in your ideas."

"How about some fruit, Mama," Abe suggested, as if to cover up any embarrassment caused by Papa's remark. Soon everyone was busy peeling oranges and apples with the pearl-handled knives. Business was now put aside, and Mama made inquiries into the health and condition of my aunt and the children.

When Uncle finally left, Papa said, "You know, Fannie, for a smart woman you talk too much. The Proverbs say, 'He who speaks much, speaks foolishness.' Now what was the wonderful idea you were bursting to tell the world? Couldn't it wait until we are alone?"

"You'd think I was talking before a lot of strangers. After all, Isie is my brother."

"Yes, and one of our biggest competitors. Maybe you forgot—but I haven't—what happened the first two years we were in business, and he was our partner. When we dissolved and he left us, he took plenty of customers with him. You'll remember, for a year I wouldn't speak to him, but you wanted peace in the family. I don't say it was his fault—all right, bygones are bygones; the boys never heard me speak of it before, but maybe it is only right they should know."

"Look, Papa, if we're to forget it, let's forget it," Harry said, annoyed that anything should be said against Uncle, whom he admired. "Now exactly what was your idea, Mama?"

"I was about to say that if instead of making a shirt like a nightgown, as large as a balloon, it was cut instead to fit closer to the body, we could save maybe five or six inches of material on every shirt. Can you imagine how much goods you would save on a hundred thousand dozen?"

Abe smiled appreciatively and Harry said, "That's a wonderful idea! You'll not only save yardage, but we'll have a better shirt."

Papa alone looked unconvinced. "It took me twenty years to perfect our patterns and train the cutters to satisfy our customers. Now I'll have to start all over again."

"It won't take twenty years to make this change," said Harry with finality.

A week later the strike was over. The workers went

back, their strike lost. Nobody rejoiced. Perhaps both workers and bosses knew it was just a truce, that the battle was sure to be resumed.

Mama kept her promise, and wages were raised. "I cannot work with people and know that they are cursing me behind my back."

The faithful were, of course, rewarded first, but the increase trickled down to the steam pressers, the folders, the swatch-makers, all down the line. The ladies' underwear department was closed, and the girls all re-settled.

Mama kept up her weekly trips to the factory and always brought home a new set of patterns. At night she would sit comparing the old patterns with the new ones. She was certain that finally there would emerge a design which would save those inches of cloth. Then the new wage increase would not only be absorbed, but as she optimistically pointed out to Papa, it would enable them to triumph over their competitors.

20

BIG BUSINESS

"*ABE IS HOME*—Abe has come home!" Emma, cleaning the basement windows, was the first to spy him, and it was her raucous call that rang through the house.

I threw down the geography book that I was studying; Sidney stopped practicing his scales, and little David ran in from the yard, pulling his fire engine after him. We jumped on our oldest brother, almost bowling him over, as he came in through the door.

"Hello, kids—hello—what's all this?" Poor Abe was a little bewildered by this unaccustomed display of affection. He gave us each a little peck on the cheek, asking, "Where's Mama? Mama was at this very moment coming heavily down the stairs, and in another minute she folded the nineteen-year-old Abe in her arms.

Abe had been away "on the road" nearly eight weeks. It was not the first trip he had made as a salesman for the firm. He had been to Buffalo, Detroit, Cleveland and Chicago before, but this was the first time he had been sent as far west as San Francisco to see old customers and perhaps contact new ones.

"Well, how was it?" we asked in chorus. "How long did it take to get to the Coast?" "You slept six nights on the train?" A long, prolonged whistle from Benjie. "What did you do when you had to go to the bathroom? What's a Pullman? Did you see the Pacific Ocean? Gee, your postcards were wonderful!" We swamped him with questions, scarcely giving him a chance to answer.

"Will you keep quiet for a minute, kids! I'll tell you everything and show you the presents I brought home. You know, Mama, I went downtown first, right from the train. I saw Papa and Harry. When they told me you were home today, I was surprised; I was afraid you might be sick. They told me why you stayed home—making the wedding for Annie. God, how did that ever happen? Did you get her the man, too? I thought she would end her days at the sewing machine as the prize old maid of our factory."

"Don't laugh at Annie," Mama said. "Annie is a wonderful girl—*nu*—call her a woman, the best forelady I ever had. She's forty years old, but she's worked for us for nearly twenty years. No one knows better than I what she is. She took care of her mother, who was nearly blind, and her father, who was doubled up with rheumatism. When, I ask you, when in these last fifteen years, could Annie have had time to even think of a husband? To you, maybe, she is homely—believe me, in my eyes, she is beautiful."

"Well, Mama, who's the lucky man?"

"You know Abram, in the cutting department. He lost

his wife a year ago; and with four small children, he was nearly going crazy. Believe me, he made plenty of mistakes in his figuring the cloth. If your father did not have a heart of gold, he would have thrown him out, not once, but ten times. What could be better? Annie has worked enough at a machine—now she needs a husband and children; so I brought them together—tonight is the wedding."

"Mama, we want to see our presents," we children interrupted. "What did you bring us, Abe? Show us the presents," and we began to unstrap the large leather cases.

"Wait, children. Abe must be hungry. I just finished cooking thirty pounds of fish for the wedding. I can spare a few pieces. You don't want anything? All right, now tell me, Abe, how did you make out?"

He sat down, crossed his feet, took out a big cigar from his pocket, lighted it and started puffing at it before he answered, a happy twinkle in his eyes. "Well, Mom, you must have seen the orders. 10,000 dozen, 6000 dozen —not bad. Harry said I did better than Rothstone—new territory, too. But Papa, I thought *he'd* be tickled; instead he just seemed annoyed and angry. I can't make him out."

There were steps coming down the areaway. The iron gate opened. "That's Papa and the boys now," Mama said. "They're home a little earlier tonight because of the wedding. The ceremony is for seven o'clock. I suppose it will be a miracle of promptness if they bring in the *Chuppa* at nine."

"Hello, Abe." Harry and Ephie kissed him, although

they had seen him at the shop. Papa looked solemn. He nodded his head in greeting, and went to wash up.

"Emma," Mama called, "I can see the Boss is hungry. Bring in a piece of herring and a piece of pumpernickel for him on a plate. Then we'll all have a plate of soup and a piece of fish. It's best not to rely on the wedding supper. One can faint with hunger until they get ready to serve it."

"We want to see our presents," we insisted. "What did I get?" "And I?"

Everything was forgotten in the excitement as Abe opened the brown leather bags and brought out his gifts. There was an exquisitely carved ivory figure for Mama to add to her curio cabinet; some handkerchiefs of Chinese linen for Papa, who, when he took them said, "Such handkerchiefs—who can use them; they're like tissue paper!"

There was a camera with a tripod for me. I would not admit it, but I was disappointed. I examined the accompanying booklet, too distressed to pay much attention to the gifts of the others. Such intricate and complicated directions! Shutters to open, so many fractions of an inch, to stand so many feet away, the sun to be at such an angle—just so many minutes for the exposure. It was worse than a problem in arithmetic. I never was able to use it, nor was anyone else. Eventually Ben got possession of it, and with his usual inquisitiveness took it apart, studying and worrying it as a dog does a bone.

The Chinese slippers (embroidered in gaudy colors), which Abe gave me also, were much more to my liking, even though I never succeeded in getting them on my feet. But I was as delighted with them as was Emma with the silver filigree brooch, which she tucked away and thought too good to wear, even to church.

Mama was now serving the younger children their supper. They were seated at one end of the long table. The three older boys and Papa were at the other end, having a snack before going to the wedding.

"Well, Simon," said Mama, "what do you think of your eldest son—an order for 6000 dozen is not to be sneezed at!" Papa frowned, "What right has he to take it upon himself to change the price without consulting us? All of a sudden he has become a *ganzer macher* (big shot)!"

"Listen, Papa!" Abe began. "I can explain how it happened. All the drummers and salesmen from the big shirt houses were sitting together in the train, smoking, playing cards, having a good time. They invited me to join them, even offered me a cigar. They laughed at me when I said I didn't smoke. I took one and tried it. I wanted to know these older men; I felt I could learn from them."

"Sure," said Papa, "learn to smoke cigars at fifteen cents apiece."

"We got talking. Slater turned to me. 'What's the matter with you people; are you in business for your health? If it hadn't been for your undercutting our price, I could have gotten more than $2.50 a dozen. The jobber quoted your prices, and even after I knocked hell out of your shirts, I had to be satisfied with the $2.50. How long do you think that you can keep it up?' "

"So now we're going to learn our business from Slater, the drummer from Phillipson," Papa replied.

"Wise people can learn from everyone," Mama said calmly, "even from fools. Go on, Abe, finish, because I can't be late for the wedding, I'm the *unterfierer* (the one who gives away the bride)."

"Well, when I got to Chicago and saw Seiderman Brothers and showed him our line and quoted $2.50 a dozen for the white demet, he got excited and said last season he got them for $2.10. I told him that was last year, the shirts would be now at least an inch longer and have a better button. He grumbled—then said, 'All right, Abe, ship me 3000 dozen.' It was as easy as that! I knew the price was still low. In Frisco I made up my mind to get more."

"Sure," Papa said sarcastically, "and what if he cancels the whole order?"

"Who says he'll cancel?" said Abe.

"Because we can't make a shirt as good as Slater's firm. We made our name on the $2.10," Papa angrily answered, "and you know it."

Harry had been quietly making notes on a piece of paper. "I've been going to the factories, Papa," he said, "for nearly four years now, and I've done a little figuring too. Take, for instance, our $2.50 line. How can we continue to make a shirt for twenty cents, with two starched collars and a pair of cuffs—five pieces to every shirt. We must charge more. They are demanding more wages at the factories, and they must get it if we are to run at full production. What we need are more factories, greater production—better and more modern equipment."

"I suppose you, too, at seventeen, are going to tell me how to run the business," Papa said angrily. "When your Mother and I started twenty years ago, we did very well without your help and advice—we started from nothing —cutting in one room and selling the goods ourselves."

Mama broke in. "Look, let's put an end to these arguments. Twenty years ago was one thing, today it's another. One has to move with the times. The boys are young and ambitious. Isn't that what you want? Do you want to be like Landauer, who drove his sons away? What are we building for, ourselves or for them? Not that you are not right in one way—as the head of the business, they must consult you for changes. But they are right, too—they are not afraid to make changes in order to forge ahead. Come, let us not make mountains out of molehills. Tonight it's Annie's *simcha* (happy time); we must go and rejoice with her."

Suddenly everyone seemed content. Papa shrugged his shoulders, his good nature restored. "Your mother!" he said as he turned to the boys with a smile. No words of praise came from his lips; he just let us feel that he knew she was wonderful.

21

MAMA TAKES A HAND

BICYCLES HAD just come into vogue and cost a fabulous amount of money, more than a hundred dollars each. The arrival of a bicycle for Drucilla Adler made a sensation on our block. None of us was too proud to beg humbly for a ride. The bicycle was unbelievably heavy, and it took at least two of us to hold it while the novice careened to the left and right.

"If Drucilla can get a bicycle, why can't I?" I asked my parents one day. I begged and begged, but the best I could wangle, for all my nagging, was a tricycle. "Bicycles," Mama said, "are not only too expensive, but they are dangerous, especially for girls!"

Harry and Ephie were more successful. "They work all day," Papa explained, "and deserve to have fun and exercise."

On Saturdays and Sundays our neighborhood had the appearance of a circus. Down the street the boys came riding on their two-wheelers, one behind the other, pedals

working furiously, arms crossed on their chests, on their
faces a devil-may-care expression that seemed to say,
"Look at us, we ride no-handed!"

We girls gasped at their daring and encouraged
further feats of valor. One boy, to please us, rode facing
backwards, another used only one foot, then threw the
other foot nonchalantly over the handle bar as a brewery
truck or an ice wagon thundered by. Is it any wonder,
then, that I showed little enthusiasm for my tricycle,
which could only be ridden on the sidewalk, with no possible hazard other than occasionally bumping into a luck-
less passerby?

I discovered Central Park when Papa decided to get a
horse and carriage and took us there. Papa loved outings
to the country, and a drive to the Park seemed a reason-
able substitute. Perhaps it was Mama who made the great
decision to buy "the trap," as the carriage was called,
but it was Papa who drove the horse, a large, boney,
brown animal. All week Jigger, as we affectionately called
him, was used at the shop for making short hauls in a
light wagon, but he was very amiable and adjusted very
nicely to his more stylish rôle of pleasure horse on Sunday
afternoons in the spring and early summer. Papa sat in
the front seat, Mama next to him, and as many of us as
possible squeezed into the back seat. We took off, surrounded by a sizable crowd of our young friends, who
waved us goodbye as if we were setting out on some
perilous adventure. Papa held the reins firmly in his left
hand. The whip, nicely poised in his right, he rarely used
except to discourage Jigger from making straight for
the stable.

The trap was a two-seater that at a pinch could accommodate six of us. It was without any covering overhead and if it rained while we were out driving we pulled out some sort of waterproof material concealed under the seats for such an emergency and opened a huge cotton umbrella for further protection.

Carriages were not altogether a novelty on our street. Doctor Adler who lived a few doors from us had a coachman drive him to his calls in a shining black coach. His only child, Drucilla, a girl about my own age, thin and freckle-faced, frequently accompanied him, especially after her mother died. Then there was Lillian, the daughter of a famous actress, who frequently passed us as she drove along in an elegant brougham. We stared in wonder as she sat stiffly among the cushions of the big carriage, looking exquisite and fragile. Often she had the coachman walk the horses, and sometimes stopped them altogether so that she could watch us play. We thought of Lillian and Drucilla as rare beings who lived in a different world from ours, rich beyond anything we could imagine and, therefore, marvelously happy. It was perhaps twenty years later that I met these two princesses of my childhood, and only then did I learn how bitterly lonely their childhood had been.

But bicycles and tricycles and even the horse and carriage could not keep Mama and Papa from feeling that it was time for them to move uptown. They could no longer close their ears to tales of gangsters grown so bold as to invade streets adjacent to our own respectable East Broadway. It was even whispered that Jewish boys had become regular loafers and had gangs of their own like the Irish and Italians, and it seemed so much more shameful to us that they were Jewish. Then there was the problem which I presented. Mama feared that I, too, might become "wild," God forbid! "Wild" implied anything from going about unkempt to a too friendly acquaintance with boys.

There were other reasons, too. Education was a word now begun to be used more and more in our home. The three older boys had their careers mapped out for them at the shop. "As for the others," Mama said, "there will be no need to hurry them to work, as the older ones have been hurried. They shall have an education, go to college, study whatever is closest to their hearts. Ben and Sidney already say they want to be engineers! So let them be engineers. We must move uptown!"

But we actually did little about moving. The ease and convenience of going to and from work made my parents hesitate. When still another family with background similar to ours would move away to the seclusion of Flatbush or upper Manhattan, Mama would again remember her dream to provide something better for the younger children. "Simon, we must look for a house. The future is safe. Abe is a crack salesman now and travels into every corner of the United States with his samples. Harry—do I need to tell you about Harry? What he knows about manufacturing, men twice his age don't know. Ephie, it's true, is on the lowest rung of the ladder. He's only just begun, and our motto is for our children the same as for strangers. 'You've got to start at the bottom.' "

The future did look secure. Then came the panic of

1893 and the two terrible years of depression that followed in its wake. Banks suddenly called in their loans and refused new ones. Business was at a standstill. Cotton mills refused to ship goods. Factories began to close. There was idleness and hunger among the workers, and the fear of bankruptcy and utter ruin among those, like Mama and Papa, who operated their own businesses.

We younger children sensed something was terribly wrong, but all we knew was that "things were bad downtown." After long hours at the shop, even longer than usual, Mama and Papa would return home at night and talk in low, serious tones with their friends. "How can we save the business?" Their life work seemed about to collapse. For many of their friends it was already too late. They were forced into bankruptcy. Some took another way out of their difficulties. One night I heard talk about Ezra Cohen, a man loved and respected by all. I caught the words, "His wife, God forbid, it shouldn't happen to our worst enemy, found him hanging in the cellar."

Mama and Papa, their faces lined with care, refused to surrender to the gloom and despair which surrounded them. They still hoped that their little edifice, built with so much sacrifice, would not fall. If only the merchant princes who now refused them goods could be made to see that they were to be trusted.

Mama, as usual, took the initiative. She announced that she herself would go to see Mr. Gibbs, the owner of one of the largest mills. Papa said, "What's the use, they call us a 'one-horse concern'—they don't care if we're forced to the wall."

But Mama was undaunted by such pessimism and went ahead just the same. Some days later she joyfully recounted, a bit boastfully, how she had been received by Mr. Gibbs, having pushed, cajoled and talked her way into his presence. Although surprised and even a little shocked at a woman's invading his office, he listened attentively as she told him of the uphill fight, by Papa and herself to get their business going, of their years of effort and self-denial. Without a note or a paper to aid her memory, she gave him the figures on how much she and Papa manufactured, the production costs, the small margin of profit, and the steadily increasing volume of orders. Would he have faith in the integrity of the firm, consider their long record of honesty and fair dealing, and give them the merchandise they could not pay for now, because of the panic and the refusal of the bank to issue loans?

Mr. Gibbs was impressed by her grasp of financial matters and her grit. She couldn't help talking of her family, too, of her six sons and one daughter. Three of the boys, she told him, were already learning the business. The others would learn what they liked and go to college.

"When I left," she told us, "he shook my hand warmly, called me a sort of pioneer, and said that I was blazing a trail other women would some day follow. I asked him, 'Blazing a trail? What does that mean?' He smiled and said, "You have helped to clear a road that has been closed to women, you proved that a woman could succeed in business as well as a man and bring up a family besides!' " She proudly repeated his words of praise, and she never forgot the friendship and respect he showed her. She and Papa got the needed goods, the factory started working again, and the storm was weathered.

One evening she and Papa went to see Mr. Gibbs at his home, since it was difficult for them to spare the time during the day. They told us how simple and kind he was, and what a fine house he had on East 73rd Street, "A street so quiet you can hear a pin drop." Then Papa said, "You know, Fannie, some day when we move, who knows? To live only two blocks from the park, where the streets are so clean, so quiet, and from where you can almost see the trees!"

They began their search for a house in earnest. It was early summer about a year later. Again Jigger and "the trap" were waiting to take us for a ride. The older boys had more exciting things to do. Even I hesitated, the novelty had worn off. To sit still for so long made me fidget, though I occasionally squeezed in the front seat and was allowed the illusion of driving by being permitted to hold the reins. But I didn't like to refuse, for without his saying so, I felt Papa wanted me very much to go. Mama and Papa sat in front, as usual, while the three younger ones and I climbed up into the back seat. When we reached the Park, we were happy to get out, stretch our legs and run about.

As always, Jigger was Papa's real consideration. He rested him in the shade of some trees, unchecked his neck rein and patted his nose and sweaty flanks. Jigger loved that. He dropped his head and nosed about the shrubbery and grass, nibbling contentedly. When he was cooled off, Papa led him over to a trough conveniently placed nearby. We stood there watching Jigger drink gallons of water. Cocking one eye at us, he let the water dribble from

the side of his mouth, as if to say, "You don't know how good this is!" Then Papa lifted a small iron weight out of the carriage and attached it to Jigger's bit by a leather strap. This was to discourage him from investigating a more succulent piece of turf and dragging the trap over the cement walk. Meanwhile, we played games or just rolled on the grass, except where little signs warned us to "Keep Off."

We couldn't stay very long. It was soon time to return. Instead of going through the park to Fifty-ninth Street, as usual, Papa turned at the Seventy-second Street entrance at Fifth Avenue and drove slowly through Seventieth Street. The clappety-clap of the horse's hooves made a pleasant sound in the Sunday afternoon stillness. Between Park and Lexington avenues, in front of a small brownstone house at number 122, he stopped, letting the reins fall slack in his hands. Mama was smiling, as she said, "Look, Simon, they took down the 'For Sale' sign." "This is our house, children. In September we will move in, when the carpenters and workmen are through."

Neither Papa nor Mama said any more. Perhaps they couldn't. As for me, I liked it. I wasn't greatly impressed by the house, for all brownstone houses looked alike to me—the high stoop, the double glass doors, the shining brass knobs. But the Park with its lovely lake was nearby —the lake meant skating on the ice in winter. The Lenox Library was only two blocks down the street. Once we had timidly visited it and had been overwhelmed by its treasures of painting and sculpture—now I could go there every day if I liked. Most important of all there was Normal College (later Hunter College), only around the corner. I was sure I would go there.

I nodded my head in pleased approval. Papa picked up the slackened reins, cluck-clucked to the horse, and we returned home. Back on East Broadway, all was hustle and bustle. My friends were holding the jump ropes; as they played "high water, low water," boys darted in and out of wagons or horse-car, and there were all the cheerful noises that I knew and liked—but in my heart I was glad we were to move uptown. A different world beckoned to me.

22

UPTOWN

"*HOW DO YOU LIKE* living uptown," my cousins May and Rose asked me on one of their first visits several months after we had moved.

"It's fine," I told them. "I don't mind it being so quiet anymore. Imagine when I leave for school in the morning, there's not a soul stirring on the whole block, except old Mr. Reade who lives in the brownstone house next door. He drives his horse hitched to a little racing runabout to the Park every morning, just to exercise the horse, he told Papa. I heard Mama say your folks were going to move uptown, too."

"We are. Isn't it wonderful? Aunt Rachel and Mama found two flats not far from here and they have all the improvements, running water, steam heat and a bathroom."

"Rose, tell me how do you like high school?" I asked.

"It's just wonderful. It's one of the reasons we're moving from Henry Street. The long ride on the new

Third Avenue cable car makes me dreadfully car-sick. Besides, Mama is anxious to get away from all the unhappy associations since Papa died."

The girls were eager to see the house and we made a minute inspection of all the rooms. Then supplied with ginger snaps, nabiscos, nuts and other delicacies taken from the kitchen cupboard, despite the voluble complaints and objections of the cook, we started for my room on the top floor.

"What's going on here?" May asked as we skirted beds and chairs piled on the landing of the second floor. "It looks as if you were preparing to move out again."

"No, be careful, don't knock your head against the box springs. It's just one of our cleaning days."

At the sound of our voices, Katherine, the new upstairs girl and waitress, emerged from Mama's room. She was a forbidding sight, her hair in dusting-cap, rags flung over shoulders, broom and feather duster in her hands. She looked at us grimly, "And your Mama wants to know what happens to all the crackers she buys every week!"

"We're going up to my room," I said as we continued to mount the last flight of stairs.

The girls were a little taken aback by the bizarre furnishings of my room. "What is it supposed to be?" Rose asked, not knowing whether to admire it or not. Before I could answer, May spoke for me, "It's the most perfect Turkish den imaginable. My mother was here when the interior decorator brought samples of the drapes—they're gorgeous."

"It's very unusual," Rose whispered, her doubts not quite dispelled.

"You certainly got used to living uptown very quickly," May continued. "Wasn't it dreadful not knowing a soul in your class, or even in the whole neighborhood?"

"I guess it would have been if I hadn't met Ellie Hertz. She's in my class and we became friends from the very first day. She's bright too. As soon as the teacher asks the class a question, her hand is the first to be raised. She'll be here in a little while and you'll meet her. She isn't a bit good looking; her face is all broken out in pimples which she squeezes. Her big sister told her not to worry about them, that they'll all disappear when she gets her period. Imagine, she can tell her sister things like that, things I wouldn't dream of mentioning to Mama."

"Heavens, I don't care how clever she is, she must be a sight," and May complacently fingered her blond ringlets.

"But there's one thing she has got, May. Wait until you see her hair! Her braids go *way* down below her waist. You've often noticed the enormous billboards on all the 'el' stations—you know of a woman with a mass of crinkly hair hanging down her back, and on the sign, 'Danderine grew this Hair.' Well, that's nothing to Ellie's."

May was silenced. Long thick hair in the early nineteen hundreds constituted a woman's crown of glory and Ellie had an abundance of glory.

A year had passed before I realized it. I was a little taller, my skirts a little longer and my hair turned up, tied with a ribbon at the nape of my neck as befitted a freshman at Normal College. I was studying Greek and Roman history, Latin and Shakespeare's *Merchant of Venice*. Life was wonderful and glorious. The memory of the bleak hours spent in the algebra class were forgotten, except as examination day loomed.

Although I lived only two blocks from the college, I walked those two blocks with my eyes glued upon an open book. It gave me, I thought, such a studious and other-worldly appearance, a pose I was not averse to assuming.

"Whoa! Can't you look where you're goin'?"

I looked up, startled to see the angry face and menacing fist of the driver. Disdainfully I stepped away from under the horse's nose. I continued on my way un-discouraged, but in the future, although I still held tenaciously to the habit of reading as I walked, I managed to keep a weather-eye cocked at the crossings.

I made many new friends, too many in Mama's opinion, and they all liked to come to our house where we could sit in my room and discuss life. Many serious things engaged our attention. Of prime importance was our desire to get acquainted with boys besides the friends of our brothers who habitually ignored us. Then there was religion—we spent hours discussing the comparative merits of our own orthodox form as compared to the new and exciting reform Judaism which many of my friends eagerly advo-cated. With some of the girls I joined a confirmation class conducted by Dr. Stephen Wise, a young rabbi with a deep sonorous voice, a great gift of speech and magnetic personality. It gave us girls goose pimples just to listen to him.

When I had asked Mama whether I might join this class at the 65th Street and Madison Avenue Temple, Mama said with her usual bluntness, "I suppose one can get religion in a Temple as well as in a Synagogue."

When our enthusiasm for religion abated somewhat, we became ardent disciples of an astonishing new nature cult called the "Simple Life." We flung away our corsets and stays, wore Greek sandals, and in every way possible showed our contempt for the current styles in dress and food. We flaunted our devotion to "higher things."

Mama occasionally saw my friends and gave them what I felt were critical and disparaging looks. She could not understand that their rundown-at-the-heel, careless appearance was deliberate, a visible expression of the "Simple Life."

Katherine too, the household oracle, was equally unimpressed by my friends. One afternoon as they were leaving, she remarked, "Where does yer collect them all? Now why don't yer have some refined, lady-like-lookin' girls, like yer cousins Sylvia and Mabel, instead of them gawks?"

"Katherine," I began, making a great effort to be patient, "you don't seem to realize that my cousin Sylvia is nearly two years younger than I am. Girls of my age cannot go around with babies! As for my friends, you judge by such superficial standards. Just because they dress—well—plainly, does not mean that they do not love the really fine things of life."

"Sure, I have nothing against them except that they all look as if they could stand a good wash. And look at yer own hair! It would be none the worse for a comb and brush!"

Without another word I started up the stairs, Katherine shouting after me. "Don't have me screechin' my lungs out after you, callin' yer to come down while you dawdle in that den of yours, so hurry up darlin', everyone will soon be comin' home."

Katherine, I thought to myself, is getting too bossy, but then I knew she bossed every one, even Mama.

Later I went down for dinner. Eating I considered a waste of time, unless I had a book propped on my lap which I could dip into between courses. I was deep in the story of Joan of Arc, and as usual I was unobtrusively reading while Mama carved and Katherine served from the huge platter of meat. The talk of the family floated all about me and I artfully raised my head and listened occasionally so as not to attract attention to my reading.

"Did I tell you Simon a new tenant moved into the top floor of 251. I think I've got a good janitor at last for the shanties (Mama's favorite description for her two houses on East Broadway), and he's a decent, honest *Goy* (Gentile). The floor was only vacant two weeks. But this tenant, a Mrs. Krumholz, wants her whole flat done over."

"So what's the advantage," Papa retorted. "It was only done six months ago."

"The advantage is, that it is better to satisfy a tenant than have the floor stay empty, for months maybe."

"Harry," Abe asked, "how are you coming along with the Young Folks League affair?" "The tickets," Harry answered, "are selling like hot-cakes, but I never dreamed I would have so much work putting on an amateur show."

"Brother, they sure hooked you in," and Abe clucked derisively.

"Wait 'till you see the show. One of the acts is called "Taking the Hill." We have a fellow who makes up wonderfully like Teddy Roosevelt, but you'll have a laugh when you see some of the heavy-weights who play the 'Rough Riders.'"

"It might make some more sense if you put in something about that fine bunch who sold the canned meat to our government; more soldiers died from poisoned meat than from bullets," said Papa.

"Papa," Ephie objected, "The Young Folks League don't want to think when they're out for a good time."

Papa suddenly noticed Ben cutting up a ball of twine for some mysterious purpose of his own. "Why do you waste that good cord?" Papa asked sternly. "Don't you know waste is sinful?"

"But Papa, a whole ball of it costs only five cents."

"When you know how hard it is to earn a dollar, you won't throw away five cents, not even one cent. The Talmud says——"

"Pop, Ben Franklin said it too— "A penny saved is a penny earned. He probably pinched it from the Talmud," and David smiled impudently at Papa.

Papa sighed, "You *aamhoretz* (ignoramus)! And what is worse, he's proud of it and makes jokes about it."

I didn't notice that I was left alone at the table. I was too busy reading, entranced by the vision of Joan of Arc, this untutored girl who led an army and would lead her king to be crowned. Papa's voice rudely recalled me to the present.

"Stop reading or dreaming, whatever it is and help clear the table. It won't hurt you to dry the dishes either."

Papa then went upstairs. Sulkily I helped dry the mountain of dishes. Later I appealed to Mama.

"I don't see why with two girls in the house I have to waste my time drying dishes."

"They've had a long, hard day, up since six in the morning. It won't hurt you to help," Mama answered.

"I wouldn't mind," I argued, "doing some important work, you know like my friend Eve. She's now a Librarian and she gives every penny of her salary to her family."

I carefully selected an apple from the sideboard and started to go to my room.

"That's very nice," Mama answered me. "It happens that at present we don't need you to work in a library, but you can help in your way too. I forgot that tomorrow is the tenth of the month. Help me check over the charge accounts."

Mama folded the lace center-piece and lifted the cut-glass fern dish from the table to the sideboard. She began assorting the bills. I tried to think quickly of some excuse to escape.

"I haven't finished my homework and I've my practicing—"

"Sit down, sit down, I won't keep you long."

Mama placed the whole pile of bills next to me. The first one, I noticed, was from Bloomingdale's. I hated the sight of the whole neat pile, but that one above all. Bloomingdale's was nearby and I often went there to shop. I was determined to rattle off the items as fast as possible.

"One dozen sheets, one dozen pillow cases, six half-gallons chow-chow (a peppery pickled delicacy which my bothers consumed in large quantities), one dozen cans sardines, one dozen cans salmon, one dozen social teas, one dozen nabiscos, two yards black velvet ribbon, five yards baby ribbon, one package hairpins, one package safety pins. . . .

"How many times must I tell you," Mama sharply interrupted, "not to charge such trifles. Hairpins, safety pins, velvet ribbon, baby ribbon, why don't you pay for them?"

I mumbled something about not having any money along whenever I happened to be in Bloomingdale's. I continued to drone away, "One dozen huck towels, one belt."

"Belt . . . belt?" queried Mama. "How much is the belt?"

"Two dollars and fifty cents."

"I don't remember buying a belt. Did you buy a belt?"

"As I made no audible reply, Mama said, "Put a mark next to that item, I'll have to make a complaint about it at the store."

I read on and on from the interminable list, knowing only too well that I would have to confess, before I finished the bills, that I had bought the belt.

Mama was signing her name to the last of the checks. "Mama," I began, "about the belt. I bought it as a birthday present for Eve." Mama's pen remained in midair. I noticed she had only completed Fanny, written in funny crumpled letters.

"What didn't you say so right away?"

"I don't know, I thought you would be angry at my spending so much.

"It's your keeping it secret that makes me angry. Some time, when you're not in such a hurry, I'll tell you the story of Tillie, the light-fingered one—she too wanted to be a benefactor with other people's money."

"Mama, the girls I know get an allowance every week. Why shouldn't I get one? Then I could pay back, little by little, what I owe for my present."

Mama looked thoughtful. "I don't understand. I should give you money so that you can pay me back? Very well, let it be as you say. You'll get fifty cents every week, and you'll please pay for those hairpins and other trifles. When you go to the matinee you'll get another fifty cents. Let me see how much you'll manage to save for presents."

I bounded up the stairs, relieved that I need never again follow the wretched example of the kind-hearted but light-fingered Tillie!

23

AN END AND A BEGINNING

LONG BEFORE July first arrived, many houses in our neighborhood were boarded up for the summer. Some had caretakers in the basement with whom we got acquainted. We went by day after day, inquisitively peering at them as they sat in the areaway of the deserted houses. They seemed glad of any break in the dull business of caretaking and were not a bit loath to answer our idle questions about the absent families.

In spite of our nearness to the Park, we found that Seventieth Street could be as hot and uncomfortable as East Broadway and considerably more desolate. Mama undertook to persuade Aunt Belle to forsake the Catskills and join her in a hunt for two suitable cottages at some Long Island beach.

"Israel could spend a more restful summer if he didn't have to drag himself every Friday afternoon on the Husband's Special and return late Sunday night just as tired as he was before. If you had a cottage at Arverne or Edgemere he could be with you and the children every night, take a dip in the ocean in the morning and still be in time to make a seven-ten train."

That argument proved conclusive. They rented two cottages less than a block from the beach and were so enthusiastic about the unbelievably cool breezes that swept in from the sea that they determined that summer to find a plot of ground and build two permanent dwellings and thereby end their summer migrations.

It was during one of the summer hot spells that Mama brought Grandpa out to stay with us. Both looked wilted and bedraggled as they alighted from the fringed-topped carriage which brought them from the station, but Grandpa seemed greatly changed. His shoulders drooped wearily, his reddish beard was straggly and his eyes blood-shot and listless. I felt a great sadness at seeing him suddenly grown so feeble. Only a few weeks before he had been to our house and, as they so often did, he and Mama played a game of pinochle. I enjoyed watching them. Their faces were masks of indifference as they played their hands slowly, methodically, until Zadic, with ill concealed triumph, slapped down his card and trumped one of Mama's. He gloated over his victory. Papa, who pretended to be reading his newspaper, shook his head over such childishness. He did not know one card from another, and what is more did not want to know. If it were not that his irreproachable Fannie was also an occasional card-player, he would not have controlled his contempt for all such wasters of time.

But now it was evident too all of us that Mama was worried about Grandpa, even as she scolded him. "You could have been here for weeks already," she said. "But with plenty of good chicken soup, especially with a raw egg beaten into it, and this good salt air, you will get your strength back."

"Come, Zadie," I begged, after he was with us several days, we'll go to the boardwalk and sit on one of the benches. It is so fine and clear you will be able to see Sandy Hook."

Slowly as I walked, it was now Zadie who had difficulty in keeping pace with me, even as I a few years before had strained to match his long stride. The walk to the boardwalk was soon abandoned for a rocker on the porch. Finally he was put to bed, while he denounced the young doctor, an *Amerikaner*, a *gournicht* (a nobody) who thus interfered with his liberty.

It was therefore a shock when some few weeks later Zadie passed away peacefully during the night. "He asked to see you," Mama said, "but I thought it best to let you sleep."

A lump was in my throat. This was what was meant by dying. Someone dear to you was taken away from your living world and you never, never could see or speak to him again.

The funeral was the next day and it was taken for granted that I would stay home with the younger brothers.

"I'm going too," I told Mama.

"There is no need for you to go. You have time enough to visit a cemetery."

"I'm going, Mama."

No more was said about my staying home.

We stood fifteen or twenty of us beside the open grave where, amid prayers and chanting, the plain pine coffin was lowered into the deep dark earth.

I looked furtively about me, at the tall gray tombstones with Hebrew letters cut deep into the stone and at the base the inscription, "To a Beloved Mother, To a Beloved Father."

Mama and Uncle were standing before the rabbi, who was reading a Psalm of David. When he had finished he cut a gash into Mama's black dress and into Uncle's vest. He handed Uncle the spade. There was a loud ugly thud as the dirt fell upon the coffin. Mama then took the spade and again there was the sound of earth falling upon the boards. Others now took their turn as if performing a sacred duty while the rabbi prayed unceasingly. There was now only the soft sound of earth falling upon earth, until all was covered and only the brown stain against the surrounding grass revealed the place where Zadie now lay.

"*Yisgadol, ve Yis Kadash,*" Uncle repeated the words of the memorial prayer he would recite morning and evening for a year. I read the English translation. "Magnified and sanctified be His great Name in the world which He hath created."

It was over. We walked slowly to the waiting carriages. I found myself sitting next to Uncle. "Uncle Isie," I asked, "why did the rabbi cut your suit and Mama's dress?"

"It is hard to explain, because the tradition comes down from the Bible. When a messenger came to David telling him of the death of Saul and Jonathan on the field of battle, thinking the news would give David pleasure, David rent his garment in his grief. So the tearing of the garment has become the custom in time of mourning."

"I know what you mean, Uncle. It's a symbol."

Uncle patted my hand affectionately. He picked up the tube next to him and ordered the coachman to stop at a certain restaurant a few blocks farther on. The horses were going at a good smart trot and in a very few minutes we reached the bakery-restaurant. All the carriages lined up next to ours as if by some prearrangement.

I sat with Uncle as the others came in and found places at the tables. Uncle turned to me. "What would you like to eat? I'm having a swiss-cheese sandwich and a cup of coffee. Would you like the same?" I barely nodded my head. I was ashamed for Uncle and the others that they could think of food at a time like this. But I was surprised at myself with what appetite I bit into the good rye bread and cheese. The long ride, the scant lunch, the tears and the fresh air had all combined to make me hungry. Perhaps folks weren't so heartless after all.

Mama stopped at our table to talk to Uncle about the week of *shiveh* (mourning) and to inquire about Aunt Belle. She then left us to return to Papa and my brothers.

Suddenly, the memory of someone long forgotten flashed through my mind. Where was she? Why wasn't she with us? I couldn't swallow another bite.

"Uncle," I stammered, "there was one person I missed today. You know whom I mean, Zadie's wife. Why wasn't she here?"

"She?" Uncle said quietly. "She died two years ago."

A pang of remorse and bitter regret filled me. I had

not thought of her in years. And why had not Grandpa spoken of her to me? Maybe that was what he wanted to tell me at the very end. How clearly I remembered my visit to her and her tender insistence that I come to visit her again. But I had forgotten her. Tears rolled down my cheeks.

The week of *shiveh* that followed was a strange medley of morning and evening prayers and condolence visits that took on the appearance of social gatherings. Papa attended the early morning and evening services at Uncle's, but he fled from the crush of visitors as he would from the plague. I would have liked to remain all evening, there was such an endless arrival of fruit, cakes and candy, but Mama insisted that I go home and keep Papa company.

He and I sat together on the porch, rocking and slapping an occasional mosquito. I wondered what I could talk about to Papa. I racked my brain but could think of nothing. I thought of Zadie and sighed.

"There's no use grieving once a person is gone," said Papa as if reading my thoughts. "One does all that is possible while there is life, while there is hope. But to help people is not easy. Take my parents and my sister, Reba, for instance. It's going to be hard for them to get used to life in this country. They waited too long. And that boy of Reba's—she hasn't any idea how to bring him up. In the six months they are here she has not learned a word of English. Perhaps she cannot learn. You've been there a few times, how did you find them?"

"*Bubby* is darling, full of fun," I answered. "She talks to me in Yiddish and I answer her in English, and then we both start laughing. But we're learning to understand each other.

I didn't tell Papa that I found this new Grandpa strange and forbidding as he sat at the window looking hopelessly into the street. As for Aunt Reba, tall, gaunt and ugly, her tragic face filled me with uneasiness.

"Perhaps I can help, Papa."

"Maybe you can. You see, I can't ask your mother to do more. She found the apartment on 106th Street, furnished it, got them settled. She found a synagogue for them in the neighborhood. She has enough to do, I can't ask more. Besides, she has no patience with them and I can hardly blame her."

"I know. Mama says you can't teach an old horse new tricks."

Papa smiled. "Yet in the last few weeks my old father has learned to do something he never did before, and already he is a changed man. He comes down every day to the shop and helps one of the drivers make deliveries. Helps—you know what I mean. He holds the reins when the driver goes into one of the loft buildings. He gives the horse his oats, his drink of water. It is good for a man to feel that he is not eating the bread of idleness."

"But your grandmother, I want her declining years made happy after all her suffering. Reba, too, she's gone through enough. Yankel, who brings them their weekly check, told me he found the traunt officer there arguing with them. The boy refuses to go to school, and you can imagine they couldn't make head or tail of what the truant officer was talking about."

"Why, Papa, they send such boys to a reform school!"

"That would be all that's wanting! And now, your Aunt Mary writes me she wants a separation from Mr. Kramer."

"Why?" I asked in surprise. "I thought they were doing nicely since they moved to Detroit. Besides, she has three children. I think it's disgraceful! It will be a disgrace to all of us. None of my friends have a separation or divorce in their whole family."

Papa shrugged his shoulders, sighed deeply. "What am I to do? Every week her letters come begging me to bring her and the children back to New York. Anything she says is better than the life she has to endure. I spoke to my lawyer. If she leaves him he can divorce her, and then I will have another family to support. There's nothing else I can do."

I looked at my father, as if I were seeing him for the first time.

"What can I do?" I asked.

"For Mary, at present, you can do nothing—maybe later. But my parents, you can help. Go there once a week, if that is too much, then once in two weeks. Teach them American ways, what to buy, what to eat. You're old enough, you've seen how your mother takes care of her household. If they need things, a coat or a pair of shoes, ask me for the money and buy what they need. See the teacher at school. Find out where the trouble is. And don't talk about what you do. As the Talmud says, the highest form of charity is that which nobody hears about."

"Don't worry, Papa, I will take charge and do everything I can."

I thought of that other promise made long ago. This one I knew I would never forget.

It was with a zeal which must have astonished and frightened the family on 106th Street that I rushed to their rescue. Whenever I came, I threw open the windows, regardless of the temperature outside and only closed them at *Bubby's* gentle insistence that at her age she liked to be warm. Reba merely scowled at what she regarded my madness for fresh air.

I poked into every pot and gave learned lectures on the superior value of milk and cereal to bread and tea. My directions for cooking were rather vague.

And I took a firm hand with little Sol. I remained angelically patient while he bit me and threw his speller in my face. At last I went to his teacher for help and guidance as Papa had suggested.

"The school doctor examined Sol," she said, "and he believes that his enlarged tonsils are obstructing his breathing and affecting his whole system. They should come out."

At once I made diligent inquiries, found a doctor and on the appointed day marched the reluctant Sol to his office.

"Is it much of an operation?" I meekly inquired as the doctor began to examine the now bellowing Solomon.

"I would scarcely call it an operation. A simple matter. You hold him and I'll do the rest."

People make such a fuss about everything, I thought, a little proud of myself as I held the wriggling, screaming boy between my knees, my hands firmly clutching his shoulders and arms. But my courage oozed considerably as I suddenly noticed an assortment of little knives merrily boiling in a pan. The Doctor turned to pick up an instrument. There was a rending pain at my knees; my hands and fingers felt the sharp sting of being clawed. Before I or the doctor realized what happened, I found myself holding Solly's coat. The boy himself had sped like an arrow out of the room and out of the house.

"Maybe it's just as well to wait a year or two," the doctor said kindly as he put some medication on my hands. "He seems a bit wild."

When we were alone I would report to Papa the progress of events; the success of my efforts was far from spectacular, but I was happy at the close bond that developed between Papa and myself. Mama often listened to our whisperings, as if with one ear. Once she burst out, without malice or anger, merely as if stating a fact, "Show me another man who has as many sisters and brothers who are without exception all such *schlimiels!* I know that one should honor one's father and mother and provide for them in their old age. But where, I ask, is it written that you must look after brothers and sisters who hang on to you like leeches and can do nothing for themselves?"

"If they were otherwise," said Papa calmly, "would they need me? Besides, the *Gemorrah* says, 'Hide not thyself from thy kinsfolk.'"

Mama knew her limitations. Who was she to question the Talmud, the Gemorrah and a host of other rabbinical authorities. And so she held her peace.

24

MAMA HAS A PROBLEM

THREE YEARS had passed since we moved away from the cars and cobblestones of East Broadway. The past had vanished and only the all-absorbing present remained. Normal College, so eagerly anticipated, was now a reality and already giving way to my dream of attending a university. "You simply must go to Barnard," said one of our friends, himself a serious and conscientious student at Harvard. I had no idea why I must, but I gladly passed the idea on to Mama. If it was going to make me a better scholar, Mama had no objection.

My brothers went to high school, but were happy only after school hours when they could descend into the cellar and carry on their experiments in the hole they called their laboratory. It was no uncommon sight to see Katherine perched on the top of the cellar steps and calling down to them in her good, rich brogue, "For the love of God, come up out of there. I told yer mother again an' again that you two lunatics that calls yerselves scientists will be blowin' up the house one of these days and all of us in it. If I was yer mother—" The rest was lost as Katherine angrily banged the cellar door.

David alone had the leisure to torment me. Later he became the chief tale-bearer to Mama, not out of malice, but because of his keen enjoyment in starting a good fight or argument.

In the romantic language of those days, "No boy had ever darkened our door," at least to see me. Mama and Papa said little on the subject, but I knew it was an unwritten law that I was not supposed to talk to any boys except when accompanied by Harry or Ephie, and most certainly, not to invite any to our home. Recently some of my friends had persuaded their parents that this attitude was old-fashioned; that a girl of fifteen or sixteen could, with modesty, ask a boy to call, or even go with him for an afternoon's walk. But Papa refused to budge an inch. Boys, of course, came to the house, but they were my brothers' friends. The younger ones, with their everlasting hammering and inventing of some contraption or other, I ignored as best I could. The older ones ignored me.

The following summer we again had a cottage at the seashore on Long Island. I thought, now that I am past fifteen, it is time I stepped out of my little cocoon. A nice boy my own age lived next door to us. What was more natural than that I should accept his invitation to walk on the boardwalk and see the setting sun. The sound and fury which greeted me at home when he politely returned me to my porch scarcely encouraged him to try his fortune again.

I poured out my troubles to a newly discovered friend. We met on the beach where she and I were similarly engaged in keeping an eye upon the younger members of our families. It was no longer the question of my ordering them to hold onto the ropes, as I had done a few years ago at Long Branch. Now that they were skilled swimmers, my task was far more difficult. On the days Mama felt it necessary to go to business I was expected to keep them from launching their home-made canoe on the rough and tumbling waves. Mama always felt they were safe in that fragile skiff as long as she was on the beach to watch and shout at them. On the days she went to business, the boat was not to be touched, an order easily forgotten when Mama was once safely stowed on the train, speeding to New York.

"You have only three to look after," my friend Estelle consoled me. "I have six. The girls are all right, but the boys are perfect devils. And that isn't the worst. Here am I a junior at Normal, and my mother is going to have another baby—that will make twelve!"

"How awful!"

"Yes," she continued, "it's pretty embarrassing when boys come to the house. The babies come into the parlor to have their pants buttoned or unbuttoned. I needn't tell you what a mess babies are around the house."

"Of course!" I shook my head sympathetically, although our baby was now nine years old.

"Did you say that boys come to your house?" I asked, my interest in that subject suddenly revived. "Of course. That's my brother Burrill standing over there. He's a

year younger than I and is going to medical school as
soon as he finishes City College."

I looked in the direction she pointed. "Who's that
other boy standing with him?"

"He? That's my cousin Cecil."

"He's good looking, isn't he?"

"He's more than that, wait until you meet him." She
waved to the boys. "He's coming over here, I'll introduce
you to him."

"I know you," he said to me, without waiting for an
introduction. "Those are your brothers in the canoe, and
you live in the big house, don't you?"

I was delighted to think he had noticed me.

"What are you reading?" he asked me, taking my book
from me. "It seems to me," he said with a chuckle, "I'll
have to undertake the selection of your reading from now
on."

I forgot my brothers tossing in the canoe. I forgot my
new friend Estelle; nor was my absorption in her cousin
lost upon her. With her usual good humor she remarked,
"You two certainly make me feel that three is a crowd."

"Don't be silly," I feebly protested. But she smiled and
left us "to take her dip" and to drag her several brothers
and sisters from the surf.

"You think he's nice," she called over her shoulder.
"Wait until you meet his mother! She's coming down
Sunday. Come over, I'll expect you."

Everyone, in time, left the beach, except my new
friend and me. I stood there listening to him, charmed by
his manner as he talked and talked, while I interjected
a breathless "That's wonderful," whenever he paused

long enough to permit it. No ancient mariner unfolding his adventurous tale had a more interested listener.

"Do you teach down at Christie Street Settlement?" I finally managed to ask.

He shook his head. "Not exactly. We have boys' clubs."

"Oh, you lead boys' clubs?" I interrupted. I know the East Side. I used to live there. What are the boys like in your club?" I wanted to know everything.

"You must come down with me sometime," he said earnestly. "They're wonderful fellows; most of them are about my age, some are older, nineteen or twenty. They've only been in America a few years. They talk English well enough, but they hunger for the literature, the history, the romance of America. That's where I come in. We have debates, plays. I give them readings—we conduct a paper. During the day they work in shop or have some sort of job; at night they plug away at their law or medicine or dentistry. They'll make a name for themselves, wait and see!"

"And you," I asked, "what will you be?"

"I would like to write. Of course every fellow says that. I mean I should like to write poetry, but I expect to make money, too. I'm headed for the law. Yes, I must make money for a certain daughter of the rich." He smiled adding, "That's you, you know."

On Sunday, in spite of my firm intention to the contrary, I found myself on Estelle's crowded porch. Everyone was talking and laughing as I was introduced first to Estelle's mother, whom everyone called Leah, then to Aunts Becky, Rachie, Sarah, Millicent, Tante Amelia and a host of young fry. The aunts sat on rockers, on the porch steps and hung on to the porch railings. Considering their combined weight, I judged that the rails must have been strong and stoutly made.

I managed to whisper to my friend, "Which one is she, you know, Cecil's mother?"

"She's inside with Aunt Mallie, trying on some dresses. She has to deliver a speech at Temple Emanuel in a few weeks. Just then Cecil's mother appeared followed by a triumphant Mallie.

"Look Leah," said Mallie, "would you ever know this was your dress? Of course Rachie took out yards from the skirt and shortened it. Becky, your black taffeta cape gives it the last touch."

"At least the bonnet and gloves are my own," said Aunt Esther. Well, will I do for that swell Emanuel audience?"

"Darling," said Mallie, "you look so sweet and innocent—but when your caustic tongue begins to wag they'll be sorry they ever asked you to speak."

"What's it all about?" I asked my friend, now more confused than ever.

"She's defending orthodox Judaism from an attack made by some reform rabbi. "He threw down the gauntlet," said Estelle, waxing dramatic, "but Aunt Esther flung it right back at him. It's going to be a terrific meeting—all New York, Jewry, I mean, will be there. I want you to meet her. Aunt Esther, she called loudly over the din, "Aunt Esther, I want you to meet my friend Sophie. Cecil has a terrible crush on her."

Twenty pairs of eyes turned in my direction. I had only one thought, to sink out of sight. I wished I had never come.

"I didn't know my boy had such good taste. Come inside with me," she said, "while I take off these ridiculous clothes, ridiculous certainly on such a hot day."

I noticed how tiny she was, plump but not fat as were some of her sisters. Her hands were the most beautiful I had ever seen. Her face was strong and yet there was a softness about it—just like Cecil's, I thought.

She was easy to talk to. As I was leaving, she said, "When you are back in town, come to see me. I am usually at home in the afternoons working. I'm not always so surrounded. . . ."

During the next few weeks I developed an absorbing interest in sea fauna and shells, an interest which was only manifest at seven o'clock every morning. Coming back from one of these early morning excursions, I found Mama there waiting to greet me. "Usually you don't get up until eight or eight-thirty, when half the morning is gone. Now all of a sudden your are up at six-thirty and out on the beach by seven. What ails you, anyhow? You feel all right?"

"Oh, I'm fine, fine and dandy."

I knew better than to say, "Mama, I met a wonderful boy, and he has to take a nine o'clock train to New York to teach boys swimming at the dock on Ninety-second Street and the East River. I promised to see him every morning before he goes into the city. We have so much to say to each other!"

Sometimes Mama looked at me so quizzically I almost believed she guessed. Certainly, if she had stood at her window and looked upon the beach she would have seen a boy and girl walking, hand in hand, barefoot on the

sand. Sometimes he read from a little pocket volume of
English poets. The beautiful cadences rolled from his lips,
and I began to understand poems that formerly I considered dry and dull. I thought grimly of my recitation
days. Never, never must he hear me do those horrors.

He closed his book, smiling thoughtfully. "But my
greatest love is for Bill," he said.

I felt a sharp pang of jealousy.

"Bill?" I asked bravely. "Bill who?"

"Oh," and he smiled at my obtuseness, "Bill Shakespeare, of course."

Much relieved, I said, "We had him last year in literature class. We were so busy dissecting his plays I'm not
sure I even care for them. 'Was Hamlet really mad, or
was it a seeming madness? Prove your contention by
proper quotes of lines and scenes,' " and I glibly imitated
the manner of our tight-lipped instructor.

"What a way to teach Shakespeare! Why don't they
have you listen to the music of his lines, the glory of his
English! What insight he had into the minds and hearts
of men!"

Some of this love for Bill spilled over into me, and
Coriolanus, Romeo and Juliet and Julius Caesar became
dear and close companions. I was learning something
else, too, something compounded of friendship and love.
I knew the pain caused by absence, was jealous when my
friends claimed Cecil's attention. It was something in-
definable, beautiful and tender, and I was strangely
happy.

Autumn came and then winter. Our friendship grew.
On his free Saturday and Sunday afternoons we spent

hours walking in the park. When chilled and driven indoors by the weather, we went to Lennox Library or to the Metropolitan Museum at 82nd Street and stood looking at the pictures, talking in whispers before our favorite Rembrandt, Franz Hals or Corot. Sometimes we just sat talking or laughing, startling the sleepy guard in the next room.

Not being permitted to invite Cecil to our home, I gave him a description of how Mama changed the Seventieth Street house before we ever moved into it. "You see," I said, Mama felt she had to have the help of a decorator, a rather novel idea in those days, but she wanted to do the house over completely, and she knew her limitations. Nothing, apparently, was too difficult or too much trouble.

Papa thought all this fuss and bother just so much nonsense, especially when his quiet evenings were invaded by furious discussions between Mama, the decorator and Aunt Belle. Papa would rattle his newspaper and mumble into it, "Better is a crust of bread eaten with peace and quietness than—"

What finally emerged stunned us all! A Louis XV parlor, or was it XVI, Mama couldn't be sure. The walls were panelled in rose brocade, the gold furniture—the pride of East Broadway—was refurbished in delicate tapestry and damask, but just as uncomfortable as ever. On the high, vaulted ceiling, in a cloudless blue sky, cupids, holding bow and arrow, plied their immemorial trade. Oil paintings, rose damask draperies, piano and curio cabinets completed the parlor, which led into the gloomy but imposing English dining room. Mama, who had previously never hunted anything more exciting than a mouse, had spent hours selecting hunting scenes, which later adorned the walls of the upstairs dining room.

Downstairs, in the basement, was the dining room we used every day. The table, large and sturdy enough to seat a family of twenty, was Mama's particular pride and joy. After the evening meal, the top was removed and a billiard table was revealed to the uninitiated. Mama preferred the boys to enjoy their vices at home.

But all these wonders paled into insignificance beside my room. It was hidden away on the top floor like an eagle's nest, but it hadn't any of the stern simplicity of that bird. Far from it. Apparently the decorator had told Mama that every new, up-to-date house must contain a Turkish corner. Mama thought and thought— where could she put it? "I know where," she smiled delightedly, "I know where it will be perfect! My daughter's room on the top floor."

Thus it came about that my bed was a divan, broad and luxurious. Over it hung a canopy of rich Persian stuff, of lovely blues and greens. Draperies of the same material hung in thick folds at the side, looped up gracefully, but effectively kept out the air and blotted out whatever sun managed to creep through the murky skylight. Little tables of wood and mother-of-pearl were placed at certain strategic points; each carried a delicate long-spouted copper coffee urn and diminutive cups. Dull brass lamps were suspended from the ceiling. It all had a really warm and seductive air, but was not particularly conducive to the mastery of algebra or Latin. It had other limitations, too. Neither my friends nor I could make any unpremeditated move without causing a major disaster.

But I adored hearing Mama's friends and visitors gasp their delight as they arrived, panting and breathless, on my landing. "Oh, it's wonderful, Mrs. L.! Any Turk would be perfectly at home in it."

Cecil and I both laughed.

"But are *you?*" he asked.

"Oh well, after a fashion. It is my own room, and that is really something!"

As time passed it was inevitable that Mama should guess something of my state of mind and that it should puzzle her. Lovely little volumes would come from Brentano's or Scribner's, addressed to me. Mama opened them, glanced at the title, then at the card, and then grimly proceeded to stuff both card and book into the kitchen stove. Usually they were rescued by Katherine, only slightly marred by their short sojourn in the kitchen range. Mama, naturally thrifty, was careful to thrust them where they would not too easily catch the heat of the glowing coals. She would then stalk out of the kitchen, half expecting the subsequent rescue.

What a howl I set up when an exquisite little half-morocco volume of Elizabeth Barrett Browning's *Sonnets from the Portuguese* met this fate! I was too upset to hide my tears of anguish. It had cost Cecil nearly a week's wages, and he had skipped his lunches to buy me that birthday present.

"So what is the excitement," Mama blandly inquired. "A book scarcely bigger than my hand, and all it says is 'I love you, I love you, I love you!' You've got plenty of time for such things."

Mama realized she had a problem. Her daughter was in love with a penniless, struggling boy. (True, he was of excellent family, but that was beside the point.) This was not the match she had hoped for, and the only way to put an end to it was by a firm, unrelenting opposition.

One Saturday afternoon while Cecil and I were walking aimlessly in the Park, we suddenly came upon Mama face to face. She was on her way to visit Aunt Belle, and though we were rather frightened, we timidly offered to accompany her. This was actually the first time she had met Cecil, and I introduced him, mumbling incoherently, "You've heard of his mother; she's famous. Her *Hearth and Home Essays* was published by the Jewish Publication Society, and she's a wonderful speaker."

"I know all about his mother—who doesn't?" Mama interrupted my faltering eloquence. "Every Jew is proud of her." Her keen eyes ran up and down Cecil's figure, his slightly worn suit, his thin sensitive face. "What does your father do?" she inquired, as we slowly walked westward, Mama now between us.

"He's a Wall Street man," Cecil said. "At present, he's down, but not out," he added half jokingly.

"Wall Street!" Mama's face indicated her strong disapproval. "And you," the inquisition continued, "what do you do?"

"I hope to enter law school in a few months."

"A lawyer! I know lawyers—after ten years, they're still starving."

After a little while Mama seemed more friendly, and

we talked pleasantly of many things. By the time we left her at Aunt Belle's door, her good humor was quite restored. We stood on the street and looked at each other with shining eyes. We had met the enemy and she was ours. But we didn't know Mama! That was only a preliminary skirmish in her campaign. There were various ways in which she kept herself informed of the progress of events, but her most dependable and regular source of information was David.

It was nearing the end of winter, but the ice in the park was still hard and safe. I raced home the two blocks from Normal, picked up my skates, and hurried over to Central Park. I saw Cecil standing there, stamping his feet, his hands in his pockets to keep warm.

"I didn't think you'd be here," I said, too flustered to hide my pleasure.

"I cut the last class. You're responsible for a scholar lost to posterity." He knelt on the snow, tightened my skates and my ankle supports. As we skated off arm in arm, I caught a glimpse of David who had been standing nearby and who, judging by his face, had missed nothing of the tender scene.

That night at dinner (we had discarded calling it supper since the advent of Katherine) David brightly remarked, apropos of nothing at all, "Guess whom she was with all afternoon?"

Conversation ceased. Papa stopped telling us about the vagaries of the new salesman who was now getting the unheard of salary of ten thousand dollars a year. Harry, seeing Mama's displeasure, flushed an angry red. Ephie who had become my accomplice, now seemed absorbed in his food.

"He," said David triumphantly, for Cecil's name was never mentioned.

Abe, sensing a family dispute, hastily got up from the table. He was deeply in love with his Hannah and went courting her night after night. He had no time to waste. He picked up his box of Huyler's candy from the sideboard and left his apple pie untouched—another tribute to Hannah. Mama gave him an encouraging smile, and as he was at the door, Ben solemnly called after him, "Why don't you pop the question tonight, Abe?"

Mama now turned her attention to me.

"How many times have Papa and I told you, we don't want you to see that boy again! What does she see in him anyhow?" This rhetorical question was addressed to the whole table. "It isn't as if you never went anywhere. Your brother Harry takes you to the dances of the Young Folk's League—there were at least three of them this year. With Ephie you go to the lectures at Dr. Grossman's Temple on Friday nights. On Sunday nights he takes you along to the St. Nicholas Skating Rink. What more can a girl of sixteen want?"

"Going on seventeen," I corrected.

Ephie swallowed hard, nearly choking. I maintained my stony, maddening silence as I looked covertly at him, my unwilling, unhappy accomplice. Ephie and I would start out alone for the rink, but always by some happy coincidence, "he" too was there. Ephie was delighted; he was free from the necessity of skating all night with his sister. He had found a girl of his own and could be with her. The

music played, the ice was flawless. Cecil and I skated in long rhythmic strides, our arms close, scarcely speaking. At ten-thirty we sighed, looked at each other . . . . and I went home with Ephie.

"Look," said Mama, exasperated by my silence, "look how she sits there, obstinate as a mule, and doesn't answer a word."

I looked up. "What do you want to know?"

"We ask you, what do you see in him? He isn't even good looking, and heaven only knows when he'll earn enough to keep himself in shoe leather."

"He earns money now, besides going to law school," I answered angrily. "Besides, I don't care about money."

"You talk to her, Simon. She can't get it through her head that we mean it only for her good."

Papa cleared his throat and tried to look as outraged as was expected of him. "You say you don't care for money. That's because you have never known the need of it, have never had to struggle to make a dollar. Could you earn any?" I shook my head. "All right, maybe your friend does earn fifteen dollars a week. Do you think you could live on that?"

"And his father," Mama burst in, not at all content with Papa's mild rebuke, "he's a gambler, that's what he is."

Papa looked really shocked. Next to thieves, he hated gamblers. "No he isn't," I answered back. "He's in Wall Street."

"*Nu*," said Mama, "what's the difference, I'd like to know. They're worse. They gamble other people's money, besides losing their own."

I swallowed hard, then said, "I hear Abe talking often enough about a cotton market and buying and selling. Then there's a wheat market—Frank Norris wrote a book about it—so what's wrong with a stock market?"

"That's enough about markets," Papa banged the table. "Once and for all, let it be understood, he's nobody for you, and that's final!"

I left the table and went upstairs to my room. I threw myself upon my Turkish divan and had a good cry; but was more determined than ever to lead my own life.

25

TIME FOR DECISION

MY INTENTION to live my own life did not change Mama, nor did her obduracy change me. I nursed my resentment and the love and admiration which I had for my family cooled perceptibly. I hardened my heart to justify my own aloofness.

I now could no longer be sure of receiving Cecil's letters; they were frequently unaccountably delayed or lost. I fared little better with the telephone. If I was up in my room, at the first shrill ring I would hurl myself down three flights of stairs with unbelievable agility only to reach the basement in time to hear Mama shout into the telephone, as if she were speaking to someone quite deaf, "No, she's not at home."

"Was that call for me, Mama?" I would ask in a voice I tried to make sound casual. Mama looked at me in surprise so perfectly feigned as to leave me wordless. "Oh, I had no idea you were at home. It was nothing important, I assure you."

Only at Temple, on Sabbath mornings, could Cecil and I be certain to meet. He up in the gallery, ushering pious worshippers to their seats, looked down over his prayer book at me and I, sad-eyed and sorrowful, gazed up at him. The organ rolled and throbbed, the choir sang "The Lord is nigh to all who call upon Him, to all who call upon Him in truth." We sang of our love for the Lord, God of Israel, and thought of our love for each other.

As we walked homeward slowly after the service, we would plan when we could see each other again.

But there were hours, even days when I forgot I was the heroine of my own unhappy romance and lived a normal, healthy, even happy life. I enjoyed the varied curriculum at school. I became the president of the Junior Sisterhood of the temple where I was confirmed, and as a group we undertook to be "big sisters" to the children of an impoverished Hebrew and Sunday School on the lower East Side. However devoted we were to this project, we never lost sight of the main issue—to develop a normal social life for ourselves. By means of afternoon dances and other affairs, we succeeded at last, in breaking down the barriers which custom and old-fashioned European prudery had put in our way.

Accused by Papa of defection from his synagogue on Sixty-seventh Street, I gladly assumed the flattering title of "teacher" and for a time bestowed my meager knowledge of the Bible and elementary Hebrew on some thirty boys of that school.

Then there was the theater, the Murray Hill Stock Company, which now supplanted my earlier and never-to-be-forgotten love for the Yiddish theater. On the Saturday afternoons when the weather made it impossible for me to meet Cecil, I joined my friends for the matinee. There, high in our fifty-cent balcony seats, we alternately laughed or wept through *East Lynne, Way Down East,* or *The Count of Monte Cristo.* When the tension became too great we dug noisily into our pockets for the paper bag of candy and thoughtfully crunched our lemon cocoanut taffy, to the annoyance of the elderly ladies sitting about us.

But not the least of my pleasures was the new and precious friendship with Cecil's mother, Esther Ruskay. The first time I went to see her, it took considerable effort to overcome my self-consciousness. She was sitting writing at her dining-room table which was littered with a mass of papers. Plants of all kinds were at the windows and books lined one side of the wall. Abashed at intruding upon one so obviously busy, I wanted to leave immediately.

She pushed the papers from her with a sigh of relief, put down her pencil and said, "You're just the interruption I need. Come, we'll go into the parlor and Regina will bring us our tea."

That's how our friendship started. Even Regina, the little Hungarian maid, took on the aura of something wonderful. Did she not wait upon Cecil and serve his brother who was a playwright and who would soon have some of his acts on Broadway? What ailed my family? I thought bitterly. Couldn't they recognize genius?

However, I said nothing of this new and absorbing interest and brooded over the indifference of my family. At home I was gloomy and taciturn. The whole house hummed with activity. I tried to maintain a studied lack of interest, but due to my natural curiosity, I was not too successful. Mama no longer went to business; Papa had prevailed upon her to leave it to him and to the boys. "All right," she said, "you don't need me any more, but don't expect me to give up going downtown to the business and to find out how everything is going on. It's part of me. You'll get my advice, even if you don't follow it."

Although business claimed less of her time, Mama seemed busier than ever, especially with her charities. There were all sorts of meetings at our house, and she and Aunt Belle, who worked admirably together, undertook to influence the Boards of their own organizations. "The time is past," Mama told them, "when every kind-hearted woman, with the assistance of a half-dozen friends, can start a society for the orphans, for the aged, to lend money, to pay rent. Each and every society goes out to raise money. And who knows how that money is spent? I'm not saying anyone is dishonest, but money for charity should be spent as business-like as if it were for business."

Aunt Belle added a more persuasive note: "If there would be a community pocket-book, and one appeal for money would be made instead of this constant begging from the same people, we'd get more money and there would be less waste."

When it was time to serve coffee, I helped Katherine pass around the little yeast cakes stuffed with nuts and raisins.

While the ladies ate as if they had fasted for days, graciously accepting a second helping of coffee and emptying the platters of cakes as soon as they were filled, Mama continued to expound her ideas. "Now you take investigating—no matter how many stairs we climb in a tenement, we still cannot advise people or even take the time to understand their troubles, certainly not the way a worker can do who is trained to do it. Sure, the way we helped people made us feel good, like the pictures you see of Lady Bountiful in the comic papers, but are we helping in the right way?"

I could see by the stony unmoved faces at the tea table that they did not agree with what they called Mama's "new-fangled ideas."

But Mama did not despair. There were more ways than one of skinning a cat. She deftly turned the conversation to her next musicale. "Guess who will be my chief artist? Gussie Zuckerman! She's going to play a wonderful program, and it's just two weeks before she gives her big concert." There was a little flutter among the ladies—and as events finally proved, they took more kindly to the changed approach to social work.

Mama arranged these monthly musicales with all the care of a Metropolitan impresario; her love of music and musicians had a chance to blossom at last. I was permitted to invite a friend, a girl, of course, and as we sat on the stiff gilt chairs, uncomfortably erect under Mama's watchful gaze, not daring to lean against the damask-panelled walls of the parlor, we found the long evening of arias, of piano and violin solos, dull indeed! The best part of the evening was when Katherine appeared, fairly glittering in black and starched white and began dispensing bouillon, chicken salad, and later ices and cakes.

But beneath this outer show of busyness and pre-oc-

cupation of everyone at home, I felt a sense of injury and
hurt which only increased with time. Cecil worked at the
settlement at night, and attended law school during the
day. I was busy studying and cramming for my entrance
exams for Barnard. It became more and more difficult for
us to see each other. It was now early June and in a few
days the family was again leaving for the shore. We spent
our last afternoon together crossing and re-crossing the
125th Street ferry. We stood on the upper deck, leaning
over the rail, the wind blowing in our faces. We watched
the boats and the churning waters, and made believe that
we were voyaging far asea.

"Try to eat something. The doctor says you are so
run down. You must eat."

"I can't, Mama, I'm not hungry." I wearily closed my
eyes and thought of that last lovely ride across the Hudson with Cecil, now nearly three weeks past. He doesn't
know why I don't write, I thought miserably. I wondered if he got that job as night-clerk at the Shore Hotel
—then we could see each other. . . .

In an hour Mama came again, applied medication,
brought an egg-nog, a cup of soup. Then she sat looking
at me. I could feel her eyes resting on my face. I knew
what was passing through her mind. I could read her
thoughts as if she spoke them out loud. "Whose love is
greater than a mother's? What happiness does she seek
except the happiness of her child?"

At night Papa, Harry and Ephie would come and take
their turn to sit with me, bringing me gifts of candy or
a book, always accompanied by words of advice and

admonition along the well-known pattern of the wisdom of parents and the foolish obstinacy of children. I was glad when they left the room and I could pursue my own daydreams undisturbed.

Another knock at the door. Now it was Aunt Belle who gently but firmly took up the family refrain. My Aunt and Uncle had built their summer house next to ours. Mama had not only strong allies in Aunt and Uncle, but they were, it seems, ever on hand to press home her point. My young cousins were all solidly on my side. They were my only champions, but, alas, discreet and silent ones.

Uncle came in the late evening and took the chair so recently vacated by Aunt Belle. He was no longer tired from his long day in the City. He had enjoyed his swim in the ocean and a good dinner with his family.

As if it were an orchestral piece, he again took up the theme, repeating what Aunt Belle had said. His voice was calm and gentle, he stroked his moustache thoughtfully, as if to give emphasis to his words. "I can't understand, my dear, how a sensible, intelligent young girl like you can set herself against the wishes and judgment of her parents and indeed the whole family. And it isn't as if they were unreasonable. All they ask is that you should give up seeing this boy—I mean, for a year or two," he hastily added, as he saw the expression on my face. "Let him show that he can make something of himself, then they will see. Isn't that fair? Why don't you try to please everyone, make everyone happy. Write this Cecil a letter —let him work, to show that he can support himself, let alone a wife. In the meantime, you will go on with your college and meet other people. There are plenty of fish in the sea. Why, your Mama is now willing to let you go with that group of girls to Europe this summer. They're not leaving for three weeks; so get well and you'll be able to go. Remember, just write a nice letter to explain things. He's sure to understand and think it very sensible."

There was an endless procession of food and delicacies to my room. I hadn't been sick in years, I was touched by so much love and attention. What's the use, I thought, I just can't go on fighting the whole family. What does my little dream of happiness amount to, I thought drearily, looking at the walls of my room. If giving him up means so much to them, then I'll write the letter—but never will I say to him, "go, be a success first, then come to get me." No, I will never be as low as that. If you can't work with your boy and help him to rise—Mama's a fine one to give such advice—she didn't wait for Papa to be a big successful businessman; she started right out with him. But I don't care any more, I'm too tired of all these arguments.

That night I wrote the letter. Many tears dropped on the closely written pages, while Mama tactfully waited in the next room for me to finish. Then, accompanied by Papa, she walked to the post-office to mail it herself.

In spite of myself, I began to improve, and in a few weeks was well enough to go to the post-office to call in person for the letter which I daily expected, but which never came. He has certainly taken it in the proper spirit, I thought to myself, none too pleased with the turn of events.

One day, as I made another visit to the post-office, instead of finding a letter, he was there, smiling and grinning. Both of us were strained and self-conscious in the presence of the other boys and girls, who were slyly watching us.

"I've come every morning for the last ten days," he said, "hoping you'd be here. I wanted you to know I got the night-clerk job at the Hotel—I have nothing to do all night but write you letters." I shook my head, glad, yet worried. "When are you supposed to sleep?"

Without further words he took my arm and we began to walk to the beach. This isn't right, I thought, after what I promised Mama.

I cleared my voice, "Did you get my letter?"

"Yes, of course," was his smiling answer. I was puzzled by such callous indifference.

"But you don't understand. I promised my family that I wouldn't see you for a year at least."

"Rubbish," he interrupted brusquely. "You don't think I'm going to pay any attention to such nonsense. We are going to work out our own problem, without their help or interference. Next year I pass my Bar. I'll get a clerkship and continue working at night at the settlement. We'll manage."

When the truth became known to my outraged family, I could only admit rather sheepishly that I had changed my mind.

Miss Cannes and her select group of young ladies sailed for a six-week tour of Europe's capitals, as scheduled— but without me.

However, I had compensations undreamed of by Mama and Papa, Aunt and Uncle. Cecil's mother, to escape the heat of the summer, had, with a few other adventurous souls, secured the right to camp on a fine stretch of deserted beach not more than two miles from our house. Two grand tents were purchased, wooden platforms set down, a well dug, a cook-house built for Regina, an out-house put up at a not too convenient distance. "Camp Walden" was launched, the summer abode of Esther Ruskay for the next few summers.

She gloried in her freedom to enjoy the sight of the ocean, the sharp tang of salt air, the sun and the mists, even the storms that threatened at times to blow them into the sea.

"Who is occupying all the beds?" I inquired, as I poked around, surprised at the comfort and cosiness of the camp.

"The three cots in the round tent are for my three boys, Burrill, Everett and Cecil. I don't expect my husband to be much of an overnight guest. He's worse than Regina when it comes to storms. Besides, he would be miserable if he couldn't stay up half the night inventing a system to beat the Wall Street game."

"You mean there is such a thing as working out a system?"

"No, of course not, but hope springs eternal. Everett and Burrill will come down every night and of course, I expect *your* young friend will be a very steady visitor." We both smiled knowingly as we entered the big square tent.

"Mallie and I occupy this one. As you see, it is also dining-room and parlor."

I looked around. A rug on the floor, Indian prints on the divans, a brass oil-lamp on a table covered with a cashmere shawl and a piano—yes, a small battered upright stood in the corner.

"Camp Walden, indeed!" I shook my head in mock solemnity. "Do you think Mr. Thoreau would approve of all this grandeur?" I waved my hand impressively in the direction of the piano.

"Considering the number of keys that are missing," she laughed, "I think he would. But six weeks without any music would be unbearable."

"Do you think you could play something for me now?" I asked.

"I always feel like playing."

Even on that banged-up relic, her playing of Chopin's études and nocturnes was delicate and lovely.

It was a wonderful summer for me. Many of the people I had met in her home in New York now found their way to Camp Walden. Sarah Lyons, tall and stately and very, very ancient, I now discovered was wonderfully good fun in spite of her being a pillar of the aristocratic Portuguese Synagogue.

There was Selina, beautiful and witty, wife of Judge Greenbaum and Esther's closest friend. I met again the heavy-set, but charming and vivacious Mrs. Schechter who with her husband and family had lately come from England. Professor Schechter had left Oxford to become the president of the Jewish Theological Seminary of America. When I met him, his barbed wit and overpowering scholarship kept me cowering in my corner. There too, I met the lovely English wife of Professor Israel Friedlander, another luminary attached to the seminary. I felt small indeed as I listened to the jargon of Hebrew literature and world events which were the theme of so many of their animated conversations. But it was a friendly and warm atmosphere in which very gradually I began to feel at home.

There were days when there was neither laughter nor joy at Camp Walden. Esther sat there grieved and enraged at the news that came to her from Russia: pogroms, the Kishenoff massacre. She and her friends arranged meetings, got up petitions, wrote letters, left no stone unturned to get our government to protest against the brutality of the Czarist regime.

"Only Palestine will serve our need," she said.

"I've just finished this poem and will send it to the papers." She read it to me and as I walked home along the beach I found myself repeating some of the lines.

> Jerusalem! Jerusalem!
> Thrice welcome day
> When to thee,
> With bated sigh,
> And eager eye,
> The chosen ones shall once more hie
> To build a new Jerusalem!

26

MAMA MEETS THE ISSUE

IT WAS NEARING the end of the college year. I was no longer the shy and timid freshman, scared of the sophomores and intimidated by the juniors.

On a glorious sunshiny day in April, Cecil met me outside the college gate. He had passed his Bar, two distinguished judges had testified to his character, and we were out to celebrate. We went over to the Claremont, that enchanting restaurant overlooking the Hudson, and gorged ourselves on hot chocolate and sardine sandwiches. We talked and talked.

"Where does one get clients?" I innocently asked.

Cecil shook his head. "Darned if I know. Of course there are political clubs; you become a party horse and in time you get rewarded. But that's not for me. My boys in the settlement will be my first clients—but what they will be able to pay is another matter. Certainly nothing much now, but in time. . . . That's how to build up a practise."

"But to get back to us. This sort of thing cannot go on. We're not children any longer, to meet on the street like homeless waifs. We're going to become engaged and I'm going to go down to tell your father—beard the lion in his den and tell your folks. We'll wait, I'm not unreasonable. We'll wait two years, if necessary. I'll hold on to my settlement job, but by that time we ought to be able to get married. What do you think?"

"I'm going to leave Barnard," I said. "It's not a sudden decision. I've given the matter some thought. I don't care to teach and that's the only career that's open to me when I graduate in three years. One can get an education even if one doesn't receive a college degree."

He smiled at me. "You and Abe Lincoln, eh? But you're right, of course. But what can you do? Become a cash girl at Bloomingdale's at three dollars a week?"

"Don't be silly. I stopped in at the Community House last week to talk to my cousin Rose who is a resident worker there. She had me meet Miss Beyn, the head worker. She was wonderful and agreed to take me on to direct clubs and dramatics. They prefer college graduates, but she is willing to give me a trial. With Rose to help me, she thinks I have the makings of a good social worker."

"That's wonderful, except that it will probably be a horrible shock to your mother. She might even prefer me as an alternative. When do you plan to break the news?"

"Tonight, if I don't lose my courage."

A few hours later, I stood in our basement areaway, waving goodbye to him as he smiled and nodded his encouragement. I rang the bell and listened to its uneven jangle. As it died away I heard the sound of voices, angry voices.

I entered the hall and could distinguish the words clearly. I hesitated, as I stood outside the door and listened. . . . "Then for my part you can keep your business—Let Papa give me my share and I'll get out." I recognized Abe's voice, loud and angry. The answer came quick and sharp. . . . "That's a laugh—your share. If you think your damned walking up and down the shop when you're back from the road makes you the head of the Business you're mistaken. Or because you're the oldest that you alone are capable of solving our problems." That was Harry. Gee, I could just see him shaking his finger under Abe's nose. Abe seemed too enraged to reply. . . .

"Listen," Ephie broke in, "this sort of yelling will get us nowhere."

"Shut up, you, and keep out of this."

"Yes, you keep your two cents out of this."

Poor Ephie, trying to pacify the fighters and jumped on by both.

Mama, I almost cried out, Mama, why aren't you there?

As if in answer to my thoughts, Mama's voice rang out.

"Keep quiet, all of you. I sat here and listened as long as I could, waiting to hear you out. . . . Now you listen to me.

"You, Abe, as the oldest, ought to have more sense. Why do you say you aren't valued at your proper worth? Have not Papa and I said time and again that you are the one who got us new markets—in the South, in the West, long before we could afford the high-priced salesmen we have today? And our loans and credit at the bank are in fine shape, due to you, only to you. You have watched every new account like a hawk so that the failures from our customers have been held down to a minimum. But you, Abe, will be the last to deny that it takes knowledge of men and factories and workmanship to manufacture shirts. Goods must be bought when the market is right—I know, Abe, don't interrupt me, I know you've done your share in that respect, too. But building up one factory organization after another, is the rock-bottom of our business. Labor and costs must be figured to the penny, if we are not to be undersold by our competitors. We must produce a salable article before it can be sold. Surely, you should be the last to deny that Harry has done that. He has won besides, the love and the confidence of the people who work for us and who manage our factories. People like him and that's important in business.

"Even Ephie, young as he is, is an important cog in the machinery of manufacturing. He sits in his office, but the record of every swatch from every shirt sent to the factory is there. Style, measurement, and a thousand other details from the purchase of the buttons and the thread to the boxes and cases in which they will be boxed and shipped, all go through his hands.

"All I'm saying is that together you're like a fine piece of cloth, a fabric well woven, strong and durable. Each one has his work cut out for him, his talents. Together you can grow strong and powerful. Separate, and you are nothing.

"And who knows—need it stop with you three? Ben, it's true, is only a boy, his mind set to become a scientist. But when he's told all he knows to Mr. Edison, perhaps he'll have a little time to give us. Didn't he tell Papa about the sprinkler system and how it would reduce insurance if it ever was introduced into our factories? I tell you, I feel it in my bones, he's going to be a genius! And Sidney, so he's going to be a chemical engineer. But must all the good dyes come from Germany? Or maybe he'll invent a special starch—or something to keep the goods from shrinking.

"I say again, together you can build an industry. Thousands of people can earn a decent and honorable living working with you. Are you so foolish as to throw all this away? I won't even speak of the effort, the years of sacrifice your Papa and I made to build it, to give up what we now have—" her voice broke.

I went quietly into the room. Harry held Mama's hand, as if he were pledging himself to her—saying tenderly, "You're right, Mama, as you always are." Abe was bending over her chair, his voice a little husky, as he patted her shoulder: "It's all right, Mama, no harm done, we just blew off some steam."

Ephie was blinking his eyes as if he were holding back tears. The boys then left the room and I was left alone with Mama.

"Mama," I began, "you ought to be proud and happy."

"Why?" she asked. I looked at her, but could see no trace of the triumph I expected—only a great weariness.

"Why?" I repeated, "Your sons listened to you as if you were a judge. I think it's nice that they feel you deal so justly with all of them."

She sighed. "Yes, for the present there is peace among them. But who knows what the future holds—that's something else." Again she sighed.

"Mama, I want to talk to you. Perhaps I shouldn't bother you now, but if you don't feel too tired I'd like to tell you what's on my mind."

Mama looked at me sharply, waiting for me to go on.

I knew that I had to plunge right in. "I've decided to leave college."

"Leave college? Are you crazy—after all the trouble to get into Barnard? Why do you want to leave? What's wrong?"

"I want to earn money now, not wait three years until I graduate. I'm going to get a job as a social worker. I know it'll take time for me to learn to be a good one, but they'll pay me while I'm working."

Mama looked puzzled. "What kind of a social worker? You mean like your cousin Rose and live in a settlement?"

"I don't have to live there. Cecil and I are going to get married some day and if he cannot come to see me here in my own home, then I will live at the settlement." My voice was quavering.

"What kind of talk is this about getting married? To whom? To what?"

I gripped my chair with clenched fingers. "Mama, don't pretend you don't know. Cecil and I are engaged. He passed his Bar and he's a lawyer. He'll work and I'll work and in two years we'll get married."

There it was, all said. My heart stopped pounding and I felt only immense relief. I felt like a child who has to have a tooth drawn, and once it is out knows only a measureless content. I managed to smile a silly, meaningless smile at Mama.

To my amazement, instead of anger, threats, or a scolding, Mama smiled back. She shrugged her shoulders. "What's the use of knocking one's head against a stone wall? Six boys I have brought up to be men—who, as you yourself say, listen to me. Only you— I suppose you are what they call a chip off the old block." She laughed. "Why should I complain about you? Could anyone stop me when once I made up my mind?

"Well, my daughter, let it be with happiness. You don't have to leave home and you don't have to leave college. Let this brilliant young lawyer of yours call here once a week, mind you, once a week. More time than that he shouldn't be able to waste if he wants to be a success. If he has any time on his hands, let him study his law books. That's how the actor Marx made a success after he left the Yiddish stage. You remember him, they used to live next door to us down East Broadway."

"Of course he'll study, Mama. He wants to take a clerkship too, for a part of the day, to get practical experience."

"That's good, that sounds sensible. In time, who knows, even our business can use a lawyer, that is, later, much later, when he knows a thing or two."

"Mama—I—I—I can't tell you how happy I am. You're wonderful. You'll never regret it—never—never!

Oh, Mama, I forgot all about Papa. How am I ever going to be able to tell him? He was so angry the last time."

"Papa? Don't worry, he wasn't nearly as angry as he seemed. You just leave Papa to me."

I flung my arms around Mama's neck, completely happy. I had nothing further to ask of life.